WITHDRAWN FROM STOCK
The University of Liverpool

HUMAN PERFORMANCE

HUMAN PERFORMANCE

PAUL M. FITTS

MICHAEL I. POSNER
The University of Oregon

GREENWOOD PRESS, PUBLISHERS
WESTPORT, CONNECTICUT

Library of Congress Cataloging in Publication Data

Fitts, Paul Morris, 1912-
  Human performance.

  Reprint of the ed. published by Brooks/Cole Pub.
Co., Belmont, Calif., which appeared in Basic con-
cepts in psychology series.
  Bibliography: p.
  Includes index.
  1. Performance. 2. Psychology. I. Posner,
Michael I., joint author. II. Title.
[BF481.F45 1979]   153   79-4253
ISBN 0-313-21245-7

To Mary and the children

Reprinted in 1979 by Greenwood Press, Inc.
51 Riverside Avenue, Westport, CT 06880

Printed in the United States of America

10 9 8 7 6 5 4 3 2

SERIES FOREWORD

Basic Concepts in Psychology was conceived as a series of brief paperback volumes constituting a beginning textbook in psychology. Several unique advantages arise from publishing individual chapters as separate volumes rather than under a single cover. Each book or chapter can be written by an author identified with the subject matter of the area. New chapters can be added, individual chapters can be revised independently, and, possibly, competitive chapters can be provided for controversial areas. Finally, to a degree, an instructor of the beginning course in psychology can choose a particular set of chapters to meet the needs of his students.

Probably the most important impetus for the series came from the fact that a suitable textbook did not exist for the beginning courses in psychology at the University of Michigan—Psychology 100 (Psychology as a Natural Science) and Psychology 101 (Psychology as a Social Science). In addition, no laboratory manual treated both the natural science and social science problems encountered in the first laboratory course, Psychology 110.

For practical rather than ideological reasons most of the original complement of authors came from the staff of the University of Michigan. As the series has developed, authors have been selected from other institutions in an effort to assure national representation and a broad perspective in contemporary psychology.

Each author in the Basic Concepts in Psychology Series has considerable freedom. He has been charged to devote approximately half of his resources to elementary concepts and half to topics of special interest and emphasis. In this way, each volume will reflect the personality and viewpoint of the author while presenting the subject matter usually found in a chapter of an elementary textbook.

INTRODUCTION

Before we can understand the complexities of human performance, there must be a unified framework for studying it. This book seeks to aid the reader in creating that framework, by specifying the capacities that man brings to the performance of intellectual and physical skills.

It discusses the limits of man's ability to sense, attend to, process, store, and transmit information. By seeking always for the simpler components within complex skills, it points toward an understanding of human performance that allows discussion of complicated and practical tasks, such as driving an automobile, or reading a book. Each chapter builds upon the ideas and techniques introduced in earlier chapters. Arguments are closely tied to the results of experimental studies.

Man's ability to perform skilled tasks is strongly affected by practice and by the degree to which he is motivated. Chapters 2 and 3 deal with the implications of these dynamic aspects of human ability. Chapter 4 discusses the limits to man's plasticity, and Chapter 5 introduces the analytic tools used to determine how these limits operate within various skills. Chapters 6 and 7 apply these tools to an analysis of complex perceptual-motor and intellectual performance. Finally, Chapter 8 suggests a few practical applications of the ideas presented in the book.

The late Paul Fitts called the area of study represented here "Human Performance Theory." He planned and outlined this book as an introduction to it. His death occurred while the book was well outlined but still incomplete. I do not claim to be speaking in this volume with Dr. Fitts' voice, but a great teacher does provide a point of view within which students may seek to continue their work, and I have tried to finish the book in that spirit. The final details of exposition and format are mine. I am particularly indebted to Dr. Arthur W. Melton of the University of Michigan for his work in arranging for the completion of the book.

I would like to express my appreciation to many others who aided in the finishing of this book. The National Science Foundation, under grant GB3939 to the University of Oregon, provided the funds for much of the research reported here. Permission to use figures and quotations was kindly granted by the many authors, journals, and publishers whose work is illustrated. My special thanks go to a number of colleagues who read and commented upon versions of this text: Alphonse Chapanis, William Chase, E. R. F. W. Crossman, Robyn Dawes, Ray Hyman, Steven Keele, Irwin Pollack, Paul Slovic, and Edward Walker. The production of the manuscript was greatly aided by Linda Martin, Richard K. Olson, and my wife.

Michael Posner

CONTENTS

HUMAN PERFORMANCE

SKILLS OF CIVILIZED MAN

In order to survive in a not always friendly environment, primitive man had to develop basic skills. He fashioned tools and weapons from materials at hand. He learned to build shelters, to produce clothing, and to develop arts and crafts. The skills of modern, civilized man are different and more varied. Participation in a technological society requires highly developed skills. Full enjoyment of our cultural heritage of art and literature requires skill in listening, observing, and comprehending. Social skills are also important. In particular, man must learn to communicate with others and must acquire the complex social patterns of his group.

Man's versatility in developing the skills required to cope with modern living is extremely great. Depending on where he lives in the world, he will acquire one or more of the thousands of different languages and dialects. Depending on the kind of work he undertakes, he will develop hundreds of technical skills. Entirely without being aware of it, he will develop countless universal skills ranging from those required for standing up, sitting, walking, running, and manipulating objects to those required in perceiving the world about him. Yet in spite of this tremendous versatility, man's capacity is not limitless. The rate at which he acquires skills and the level of performance he is able to attain are subject to limitations imposed by his musculature, his nervous system, and the characteristics of the activities themselves.

The study of human performance, a branch of experimental psychology, analyzes the processes involved in skilled performance, studies the development of skills, and attempts to identify factors which limit different aspects of performance. It seeks to analyze complex tasks into their simpler components and to establish quantitative estimates of man's abilities in each of the basic functions. In this way, it makes possible predictions about man's capability in performing complex skills.

FEATURES OF SKILLED PERFORMANCE

Skilled performance always involves *an organized sequence* of activities. The possession of a single item of information, a simple muscle twitch or a glandular secretion, would hardly constitute a skill. However, the smooth sequence of movements needed to hit a baseball or the integration of information in playing a game of chess constitutes a skill. Thus, the spectrum of skills is a broad one and includes both the organization of sequences of movements and the organization of sequences of symbolic information.

The organization or patterning of skilled behavior involves both spatial and temporal factors. The simple act of picking up a pencil involves skill in that the movement must be precise in amplitude and the fingers, in order to grasp the pencil, must move in a coordinated way at the right time in the reaching sequence. Similarly, speaking one's name requires the modulation of amplitude and pitch of the voice in a complex temporal pattern. The writing of a name may involve the coordinated activity of as many as twenty different small-muscle groups in the arm and hand. These simple acts of reaching, speaking, and writing become so highly overlearned and automatic in an adult that it is easy to forget the laborious way in which they were originally learned as a child.

The proficiency of a skill is reflected in the accuracy and uniformity of the component processes involved in the activity. Thus, we marvel at the execution of the soloist and the timing of the supporting symphony orchestra, or at the control of the quarterback as he throws a pass to the end who is running at full speed down the field. No less remarkable, however, are the linguistic skills that we employ every day in communicating with other people and the symbolic skills that we bring to bear on the solution of difficult problems.

Skilled behavior is not just organized. It is organized with a purpose. It is goal-directed. In fact, the full complexity of sequential activity can seldom be understood except when the end objective or goal is also understood. Thus when we ask "What is he doing?" we often mean "What is he trying to do?" Sometimes the performer is attempting to achieve some goal that is just within the limits of human capabilities, as when the Olympic diver attempts a double forward twisting somersault or the musician plays a particularly difficult composition. In competitive games such as chess, the skill also involves each player's attempting to conceal from the other the purpose of his immediate sequence of moves.

Since skilled behavior requires sequences of activity, both sensory information and response movements are continually involved. Moreover, much relevant information is in the form of stimuli arising from previous responses or environmental consequences of those responses. These sources of information are collectively called *feedback*. The only response sequences free from feedback effects are those which are so short that there is insufficient time for feedback information to be processed and modify the response. Feedback is highly important whenever a skilled performance lasts for more than a second. We may often be unaware of the importance of feedback, but interference with it has dramatic results. Prevent the sounds of a car's engine from reaching the driver, and he will almost invariably hit the brake. Place a microphone immediately in front of a subject's mouth, and record what he says on magnetic tape; then, play the record back, delayed by a fifth of a second, into headsets which muffle direct airborne sounds, and ask the subject to talk. Most subjects find it extremely difficult to talk under this condition of delayed auditory feedback. They may begin to stutter or may stop speaking altogether. The importance of feedback from the muscles is dramatically demonstrated in neurological diseases which destroy certain nerve tracts in the spinal cord. Individuals with such maladies cannot walk unless they look directly at their feet. They can, to some extent, substitute visual feedback for feedback from the muscles, but without vision they will stumble and fall. Much more will be said about the importance of feedback concepts later in this book.

It is important to remind ourselves from the beginning, however, that man is not simply a robot. He does not execute by rote long sequences of predetermined acts. Instead, almost every act is dependent upon comparison either of feedback with input, so that he may determine the appropriateness of his previous responses, or a comparison of progress toward a goal with some conception of what is desired. In driving an automobile, for example, one does not respond randomly to stimuli on the road. Instead, one makes responses in accordance with some internal model which involves reaching a destination at a certain time while obeying various traffic regulations, accommodating oneself to the other traffic on the road, and adapting one's driving in numerous other ways to the immediate environmental situation.

CATEGORIES OF SKILL

UNIVERSAL SKILLS

Organization, goal directedness, and utilization of feedback are basic characteristics of skilled performance. Most of the skills discussed so far are learned. A number of basic human functions, however, appear to be innate, in that they are basic properties of the maturing nervous system. These functions include breathing, digesting, coughing, and other complex reflexive activities necessary to life itself. The components of these functions involve the basic components of skill outlined above, and are common to every living member of the human species. The designation reflexive does not mean that these functions are considered to be unaffected by learning, but only that their basic patterns are inherent in the genetic structure of man and that the learning process is secondary to them. This book, on the other hand, will focus on skilled behavior that depends *primarily* upon learning and that, depending upon his experiences, may or may not be acquired by any individual human being.

LEARNED SKILLS

It is convenient to distinguish between two broad classes of learned skills: (1) *perceptual-motor* skills, which involve responses to real objects in the spatial world; (2) *language skills,* which involve the manipulation of signs and symbols.

Perceptual motor skills can be broken down further into three more specific categories of performance: gross bodily skills, manipulative skills, and perceptual skills. Bodily skills include processes involved in maintenance of upright position and in locomotion. These processes are so taken for granted that one fails to realize that all other movements—for example, such high-level bodily skills as can be found in divers, acrobats, tumblers, and dancers—are superimposed on these basic gross bodily processes.

Highly developed perceptual skills are required in both perceptual-motor activities and language processes. The perception of spatial relationship, the estimation of speed and distance, the recognition of spatial patterns, and the identification of patterns of sound are components of many complex processes. Thus, the comprehension and production of a spoken language involve highly developed perceptual and motor skills as well as skill in symbol manipulation.

Language skills include mathematics, metaphor, and other representations people use in thinking and problem solving as well as the ordinary language of day-to-day human communications. Before the end of the second year of life, the rudiments of language, along with many other skills, appear, and provide a means by which man can acquire the cultural heritage of past generations. The ability to use words represents a considerable advance over the silent language of gestures and facial expressions, which precedes it, and which continues to develop along with it. Only later, if at all, come the highly specialized and precise languages of mathematics, science, and logic. Skill in these languages greatly facilitates the manipulation of symbols of certain types.

Among the most recent of these special symbol systems are the computer languages, which scientists and engineers use to instruct computing machines. These languages are suitable for solving many problems involving the manipulation of symbols. Since the uses to which these machines are put often resemble skills previously performed by men, there has been much interest in the similarities and differences between computer and natural languages. A good deal of evidence from research on learning and memory suggests that much of what is stored in the brain and much of the manipulation that information undergoes involves words. For this reason it seems fitting to look for considerable commonalities between the processes performed by human beings and those performed by computers. However, in a variety of ways man differs dramatically from standard computing systems. This book will attempt to specify both the similarities and the differences between man and machine.

INFORMATION PROCESSING

It has been said that the nineteenth century was the age of power and the twentieth century is the age of information. Since about 1950 the world has seen a tremendous growth in the sciences dealing with information. Of importance to psychologists has been the development of human-performance theory, which seeks an approach to the study of information processing within man's nervous system and communication between man and his environment.

Most of the skills so far referred to can be thought of as information-processing skills. Man receives information from his environment, through some form of physical energy (light, pressure, electromagnetic heat, chemicals, etc.). This environmental information is coded by man's sense organs into patterns of neural excitation (Alpern, Lawrence, and Wolsk, 1967), which are then stored (the form in which they are stored we are only beginning to understand) and result, finally in patterns of overt behavior. The emphasis on information is not to deny that energy is also involved; clearly energy must always be present to transmit information. It is merely to say that behavior can be understood more completely in terms of the processing of information than in terms of the transformation of energy.

Three forms of information-processing activities may be specified: the conservation or transmission of information, the reduction of information, and the creation or elaboration of information.

A task involving the conservation of information is one in which man's output (his speech, his writing, his motor responses, etc.) has some fixed relationship to stimulus events, so that the stimulus (which will be called the input) can be inferred precisely from his response or output. Thus when a secretary takes down dictation in shorthand and then transcribes the shorthand on a typewriter, two information-conserving tasks have intervened between the original speech of the person dictating the letter and the finished letter.

Information reduction is illustrated by the writing of an abstract of an article. The abstract summarizes the article in such a way that the central ideas are communicated. However, no matter how good the abstract, one cannot reconstruct the original article from the abstract. Information may be similarly reduced by arithmetical processes. The sum of a set of numbers is determined by the numbers; but, given only the sum, it is not possible to reconstruct the original set. Thus computing, like abstracting, involves the reduction of information. Classifying a large number of specific events into a few categories or inferring a general law from specific instances are other examples of information reduction. Thinking, reasoning, solving problems, and making decisions may all involve information-reducing processes.

The creation of information occurs when man uses his memory to elaborate upon a stimulus. An important distinction must be made here between the creation of information and creativity. Creativity may involve both the process of elaborating upon incoming information and the bringing of order out of existing information. It may be reflected both in information-reducing and information-creating processes.

THE ORGANIZATION OF THIS BOOK

This book takes an informational approach to the analysis of human performance. This approach draws upon developments in the physical sciences, mathematics, engineering, and computer technology to aid in an objective description of man's capacities. The goal is to provide an adequate psychological account of the acquisition of human skills and of their limits. Sensation, perception, memory, and response will be examined; these are processes which form the basic components of skills. It will then be possible to show how these components combine and interact in the accomplishment of more complex forms of behavior, such as reading and the control of mechanical systems. This organization is a familiar one in science, where we come to understand the complex through an analysis of the elements which combine to produce it. In this case, the elements which will be considered are in themselves dynamic processes involving patterns of goal-directed behavior.

But before we go on to an examination of these component processes we must first consider two general topics that relate man's capacities to his actual performance. Therefore, the next two chapters deal with the principles of learning and motivation in relation to skill. This discussion should provide an appreciation of the tremendous amount of learning necessary to the development of skills. The discussion of motivation will consider the conditions necessary for man to process information at maximum efficiency. Of particular interest is the important role played by feedback in determining the efficiency with which man uses his capacities.

The book as a whole deals with the following questions: What are the principles by which skills are acquired? Under what conditions does man perform learned skills with efficiency? What are the limits to man's ability to sense, perceive, remember, and respond to stimuli? How are these capabilities employed in perceptual motor skills and in language skills? Finally, how are these principles being applied to improve man's performance in familiar tasks?

Learning, as treated elswhere in this series (Walker, 1967), is a relatively permanent change in performance that can be shown to be the result of experience. The learning of skills begins even before birth. Many of the most important aspects of learning skills, seen from the viewpoint of later learning and performance, occur during the first few years of life. It is during the early years that the basic patterns of loco-motion, manipulation, and language behavior are developed. Adult human performance involves the utilization of existing hierarchies of habits; it therefore always requires the modification of existing skills. The question of the original development of skills in the young organism, which is the special province of developmental psychology, may be rather different from the learning of skills in the adult and will not be considered here.

PHASES OF SKILL LEARNING

In 1899 two psychologists, W. L. Bryan and N. Harter (1899), published a study of adult skill learning. That study has had a profound influence on our conceptualization of human learning and performance. The task was the sending and receiving of Morse code, which they termed the "telegraphic language." The learning involved, in part, the acquisition of a new set of language skills built on already existing language habits. Another aspect of the learning, however, involved the acquisition of both the new perceptual skills required to identify patterns of dots and dashes and the new motor skills required to manipulate the sending key. This combination of language and perceptual-motor skills was a fortunate one, because it meant that from the beginning of the experimental study of skills the close relationship of perceptual-motor and symbolic processes was apparent.

Bryan and Harter's work was also significant because of two of its conclusions, still widely quoted. One was that telegraphic skill involves a hierarchy of habits. The other was that shifts between levels of the hierarchy would appear as periods of no apparent improvement, called plateaus.

Subsequent experimentation has shown that they were correct in the first conclusion, but wrong about the second. Plateaus are not a necessary characteristic of skill learning. Let us first consider the evidence about plateaus then return to the more important concept of hierarchical organization.

The two subjects in the study were working in a railroad telegraphic office, not in a laboratory. This setting had some advantage, since practice could go on hour after hour for a long period of time. However, it was not possible to control the conditions of practice, and the measures of performance were somewhat ambiguous. In plotting performance against weeks of experience, Bryan and Harter observed that the rate at which the subjects received messages increased steadily at first but then leveled off for a period of many weeks. This was the plateau. Suddenly, the rate began to increase again, and a much higher level of performance was attained within a few more weeks. The investigators attributed this improvement to a progression from a stage of learning where each small sequence of dots and dashes was heard as a separate letter to a stage in which much longer sequences were heard as words or even whole phrases.

Later investigators, while subscribing to the idea of a progression from the perception of letters to the perception of words, found little evidence that improvement in performance ceases as the shift is being made. Instead, it appeared that improvement in both sending and receiving code is continuous. Much of this later evidence was accumulated during World War II, when thousands of men were trained in code transmission and several psychologists conducted extensive and well-controlled experiments on code learning. One of these researchers was Fred Keller, who continued to investigate code learning in his laboratory long after the war was over. In 1957 Keller chose as the subject of his presidential address before the Eastern Psychological Association the title "The Phantom Plateau." In this paper, which was published the next year, he cited several studies showing continuous improvement of sending and receiving. These results indicate that even in telegraphy, where it was originally reported, the plateau is not a particularly common phenomenon.

HIERARCHICAL AND SEQUENTIAL ORGANIZATION OF SKILLS

The concept of hierarchical and sequential organization is basic to an understanding of the processes involved in skilled learning and performance. The concept of hierarchy implies two operations. First, it must be possible to group events, symbols, functions, persons, etc., into categories. Second, it must be possible to specify some restrictive relationship of position, order, sequence, or probability between categories. For example, one common form of hierarchical organization is that represented by an organizational chart, with the president of the organization at the top, then vice-presidents, department managers, supervisors, etc., down to the workers at the bottom. The military chain of command is another familiar example. Associated with each level of such an organization are the responsibilities, privileges, and duties appropriate to that level. The human nervous system is also a hierarchical structure. Thus we speak of the "higher" and "lower" centers of the brain and, below the brain, the spinal cord and the peripheral nerves. However, different levels of the nervous system can to some extent act autonomously; spinal reflexes, for example, are regulated in only the most general way by higher centers.

Natural languages exhibit a great deal of organization, or structure. Some of this structure is sequential. Sequential organization limits the way in which one letter or word can follow another. In English, for example, the constraints are quite severe; less than ten per cent of the syllables account for half of all speech (Miller, 1951). Another part of the structure is hierarchical. Thus, we can identify general or specific terms and principal (independent) or subordinate (dependent) clauses. Much of the hierarchical organization apparent in language is called grammar and serves to restrict the number of possible utterances appropriate to the language. Formal systems of logic and mathematics also provide ways of specifying hierarchical relations between levels and sequential relations within levels. The distinguishing feature about these formal systems is that each relation within them is intended to have a specific and unambiguous meaning, such as equal to, greater than, less than, included in, etc.

Motor sequences, like sentences, must follow a restricted course. It is possible to begin a reaching or throwing motion in many different ways and with many different patterns of force. Once the initial pattern has been established, however, there are fewer degrees of freedom left for terminating it if the original purpose is to be achieved. The precision of a golf shot, for example, is imparted not by the arm motion that initiates the swing but by the wrist and finger action in the last fraction of a second before the club makes contact with the ball. It is the wrist motion that allows the final adjustment which may produce a successful shot. Nevertheless, the wrist and finger action are themselves determined in large measure by the way the stroke was initiated.

A COMPUTER ANALOGY

The opportunity to develop complex programs to govern the operations of large electronic data-processing systems has led to new conceptions of how skilled performance may be organized in man. The operation of such systems is governed by a program or sequence of instructions. Parts of the program may be repeated over and over again. These short, fixed sequences of operations are written as *subroutines* which may be called into play as units by the overall program. Such subroutines may be repeated over and over again until some predetermined point is reached or until interrupted by the overall program. These fixed sequences are under the control of a higher level or *executive program* which provides the overall logical or decision framework that gives the system its flexible and adaptive characteristic. In much the same way, some sequences of movement become fixed units within complex human activity. These fixed units are quite automatic, and may be incorporated as components in many different activities. The timing and order of these units will vary with different skills and provide the unique character of each activity. Learning skills involves a new integration and ordering of units, many of which may be transferred as a whole from other activities.

With this introduction to what is meant by sequential and hierarchical organization, let us turn now to a description of the learning phases that appear to be involved in the acquisition of complex skills. There are three phases, but the distinction between them is somewhat arbitrary. As learning progresses, one phase merges gradually into another, so that no definite transition between them is apparent. The distinctions rest primarily on laboratory observations of subjects learning information-processing skills and upon an extensive study based on interviews with a large number of instructors in all kinds of skills who were queried regarding the problems encountered by their students. The present discussion is based upon a much fuller one. (Fitts, 1964.)

EARLY OR COGNITIVE PHASE

Whether left to his own devices or tutored by an experienced instructor, the beginner in most adult skill-learning situations tries to "understand" the task and what it demands. A good instructor will call his attention to important perceptual cues and response characteristics and give diagnostic knowledge of results. He may also shape behavior by calling "good" any sequence of acts that at all resembles the correct one. Alex Williams* was highly successful in bringing novice aircraft pilots quickly to the level of proficiency necessary in order for them to try their first solo flight. His techniques emphasized the "intellectualization" of the pilot's task. Williams conducted detailed discussions of each maneuver to be practiced, of the exact sequence of responses to be made, and of the exact perceptual cues to be observed at each step. These discussions were interspersed with very brief flights, which were followed by further discussions. In this way, the average time to

*This learning experience was communicated to the authors personally.

solo, one of the widely used criteria of rate of learning for a student pilot, was reduced from 10 hours for a control group to 3½ hours for the average experimental group.

During the early phase of skill learning it is usually necessary to attend to cues, events, and responses that later go unnoticed. In learning a dance step, one attends to kinesthetic and visual information about the feet, information which is later ignored. Some instructors report that one of the most difficult things for many beginners to learn is to process information concerning their own limbs. Similarly, most of us are completely unable to report many of our own favorite verbal expressions and language habits, and are often surprised to hear a recording of our own voice. One of the most promising devices for use in skill training is the television recording, which enables a student to see and hear himself immediately after attempting some portion of a new activity.

The early or cognitive stage of learning, when instructions and demonstrations are the most effective, can be considered as a first step in the development of an executive program (see above, p. 11) for the activity. This stage allows for the selection of an initial repertoire of subroutines (see above, p. 11) from the available ones that have been developed previously. At this stage behavior is truly a patchwork of old habits ready to be put together into new patterns and supplemented by a few new habits.

INTERMEDIATE OR ASSOCIATIVE PHASE

The second stage of skill learning is best described by the term *associative*, borrowed from the analysis of verbal learning in Underwood, Runquist, and Schultz (1959). Underwood's view is that the associative phase of verbal learning follows a preliminary stage, in which the responses that must be made are learned and become readily available. In a similar way, during the intermediate phase of skill learning, old habits which have been learned as individual units during the early phase of skill learning, are tried out and new patterns begin to emerge. Errors (grossly inappropriate subroutines, wrong sequences of acts, and responses to the wrong cues), which are often frequent at first, are gradually eliminated.

The intermediate phase lasts for varying periods of time, depending on the complexity of the skill and the extent to which it calls for new subroutines and new integrations. In Morse-code learning most errors are eliminated by the end of ten hours of practice (Woodworth and Schlosberg, 1954, p. 813). In aircraft-pilot training, the likelihood of the student's making a fatal error has often become sufficiently small after ten hours for the instructor to be willing to trust the student on his first solo flight.

What are the crucial issues concerning the learning of skills during the associative stage? One way to get at this question is to ask people who are closely involved with such training. A talk about skill learning among a group of teachers of physical education might elicit a number of instructive practical questions such as: "In training for a race is it better to run a short distance very rapidly and try each day to increase the distance or to run the proper distance each day and try to increase the speed? Should the student be shown the wrong way to hit a golf ball as well as the right way and allowed to practice it, or should he never be told how to hook and slice? Should beginning swimmers practice kicking, breathing, and arm strokes separately or all together?"

These are complex questions and involve a number of important theoretical issues concerning the best conditions for practice during the intermediate stage. The principles discussed below do not provide full answers to these questions, but they are relevant to them.

One of the questions is about the proper scheduling of practice. Should the practice trials be massed together in large time blocks or should they be distributed, with rest periods between sessions? In the development of most skills, frequent repetition within short periods of time results in a greater depression in performance than the same amount of repetition with more frequent rests. Perhaps this effect is due primarily to losses in motivation which seem to accompany the continuous performance of a skill. Evidence on this issue is discussed in the next chapter. There is no single optimal schedule for all skills, but frequent rest periods seem to facilitate performance. This is particularly true where the skill requires much motor activity, since the tendency to practice incorrect response patterns may increase as the muscle groups involved tire.

Even more complex is the issue of the proper sequence of practice on the components of a skill. An example is the question of whether the swimmer should practice foot and arm movements separately. Koch (1923) performed an experiment designed to provide information relevant to questions of this type. His subjects were required to type finger exercises, using two typewriters simultaneously. The groups that began by practicing with each hand separately before attempting to use both hands simultaneously made faster initial progress and maintained this superiority when they went on to practice the two-hand task than the groups that began by using both hands. This result clearly favored training in the separate components to training for the whole task from the start. Experiments on tasks like playing the piano, however, and memorizing prose have tended to show whole-task practice superior to training in the parts.

These discrepant results may be reconciled by the formulation of the following principle: If the components of the skill are independent of each other, such as the typing of different passages with separate hands, then it is better to practice each component separately. For tasks of this character Bahrick (1957) has confirmed the findings of Koch discussed above. In such tasks the learning problem is concerned only with the components and not with their overall integration. When, however, the task involves synchrony between the components, such as in playing the piano or reciting a meaningful passage, much of the learning is concerned with the overall integration of the components and thus is best learned as a whole. A practical exception to this principle may arise if the components are too complex to allow the beginner to practice the task as a whole. The best plan here is to program practice so as to develop some proficiency in the separate components, choosing component processes that are as nearly independent of each other as possible and alternating between part and whole practice.

FINAL OR AUTONOMOUS PHASE

During the final phase of skill learning, component processes become increasingly autonomous, less directly subject to cognitive control, and less subject to interference from other ongoing activities or environmental distractions. In this phase, skills require less processing. This means that they can be carried on while new learning is in progress or while an individual is engaged in other perceptual and cognitive activities. Thus, a well-practiced task like walking may not interfere with talking. The speed and efficiency with which some skills are performed continue to increase during this phase, although such improvement, as we shall see in the next section, is at a continually decreasing rate.

Bahrick, Noble, and Fitts (1954) reported a study that supports the above views. Subjects were tested on two tasks. The primary task involved pushing keys in response to lights. One group of subjects was trained to respond to lights which appeared at regular intervals; the other group, to lights which appeared at random intervals. In the second task, the subjects had to perform arithmetical operations on numbers presented to them orally. Both groups were given varying amounts of practice on the first task before being tested on the two tasks combined. Early in the experiment, the performance of the two groups on the arithmetical operations was comparable. However, after more practice, the group which had worked with the regularly varying lights scored higher in the arithmetic than did the group which had worked with the random lights. In other words, where the signals in the first task were regular, practice on that task improved performance on the two tasks combined. The two tasks were independent of each other and did not require a great deal of whole practice for synchronization to be achieved. The results specifically support the idea that continued practice on a predictable activity not only renders that activity less susceptible to interference from a second task but permits the subject to allocate more of his capacity to the second task, thus indirectly enhancing performance on that task as well.

There is a good deal of similarity between highly practiced skills and reflexes. Both seem to run off without much verbalization or conscious content. In fact, overt verbalization may interfere with a highly developed skill. If the attention of a golfer is called to his muscle movements before an important putt, he may find it unusually difficult to attain his natural swing. But despite the lack of conscious awareness in a highly developed skill, learning does not cease. More rapid responses will tend gradually to supplant slower responses, so that the rate of performance will increase.

THE LIMITS OF SKILL

Man is capable of learning an almost limitless number of skills. It is now time to consider how much improvement is possible in particular skills as a result of practice. Let us present the general answer to this question first, and then the evidence.

There are definite limits to the level of proficiency that an individual may reach in the performance of any particular skilled activity, and the prediction of these limits is of major interest to human-performance theory. However, actual performance approaches these limits so slowly that it is seldom possible to say that a particular individual has reached the limits of his capacity in a particular activity. Either aging processes begin to lower the ceiling, or a gradual change in motivation occurs so that effort to improve the skill ceases. Moreover, as will be seen in the next chapter, people seldom work up to the theoretical limits which their capacities impose.

The evidence that skills can be improved almost indefinitely comes from learning curves, where performance is considered a function of days or months of practice under favorable conditions.

Snoddy (1926) was probably the first psychologist to call attention to the continuous nature of improvement in motor skills. He used mirror-drawing as the skill-learning task. The subject was required to trace with a pencil along a star-shaped path while viewing his hand in a mirror. This had the effect of reversing the normal eye-hand relations. One trial a day was given for a period of sixty days. The performance

score was based on time and errors. In order to emphasize the relatively slow changes taking place after extended practice, Snoddy plotted the logarithm of performance against the logarithm of trials.

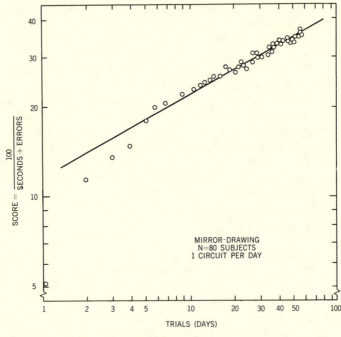

Figure 1

*Mirror-drawing. The graph represents gradual
improvement with long practice. (After Snoddy,
1926. Reproduced with permission of the American Psychological Association and the* Journal
of Applied Psychology.)

The results are shown in Figure 1. As you can see, a straight line fits
the data quite well, at least after the first few trials. This result indicates that improvement in performance continued over the entire sixty
days of practice, but that the rate of improvement slowed down over
time.

One of the fullest sets of data available on the effect on skill of
extended practice is from a field study of the time required to make
cigars on a hand-operated machine (Crossman, 1959). The data were
collected from operators whose level of experience varied up to seven
years. Figure 2 plots the speed of performance as a function of the

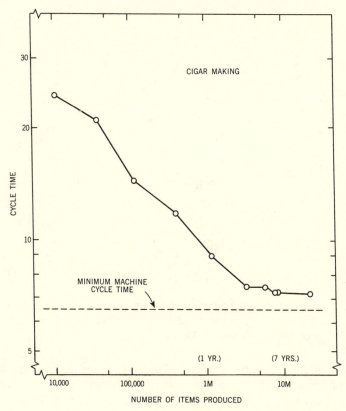

Figure 2

Performance of operators with varying amounts of experience in the performance of an industrial skill (cigar making). (After Crossman, 1959.)

amount of the operator's experience. Speed of performance increased linearly, on the log-log plot, for about four years, and then leveled off. The leveling occurred when the cycle time of the machine set a limit on the rate of work that was possible.

Robert Seibel (1963) trained three subjects in using a ten-finger keyboard which permitted keys to be activated in all possible combinations. This gives 2^{10}, or 1,024, combinations (actually, only 1,023 patterns were used, since one possible pattern is the one which employs no keys). The study extended over several months, or to about 75,000 responses. The results for one of the subjects are shown in Figure 3. Again, the learning curve is fitted by the same type of function, except that the slope of the function apparently changes at around 30,000

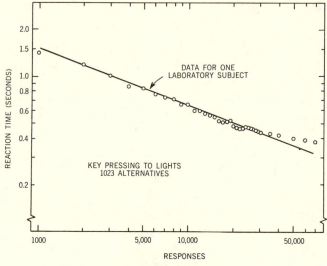

Figure 3

*Gradual improvement, with long practice, in a
10-finger key-pressing task. (After Seibel, as
reported in Klemmer, 1962.)*

trials. In his report of the study, Seibel noted irregularities in performance. For a number of sessions performance would be depressed or elevated in some unexplained but systematic manner. Such irregularities occur in most learning curves. A run of trials closely spaced in time, for example, usually depresses the results, which recover during an extended rest period. The generalization regarding long-term improvement does not refer to these short-term fluctuations in performance.

These three studies are representative of many others (Stevens and Savin, 1962), which make the same point. Performance in skilled tasks improves over long periods of time. The rate of improvement is reduced as practice continues. This relationship can be described as a power function. That is, the logarithm of performance is linearly related to the logarithm of the amount of practice. The slope of this function will depend upon the particular task.

Performance does not inevitably improve with practice. Other studies have shown that it is necessary to maintain the subject's motivation, to provide him with knowledge of results, and to take into account such extraneous limitations of the opportunity for improvement as we saw in operation in the cigar-making experiment.

The majority of published data on rate of learning concern relatively simple tasks and are often tailored to the practical time limitations of the experimenter, who may wish to train subjects for only a few hours each. Therefore, an arbitrary criterion for successful "completion" of the task is employed which does not permit continued improvement. Such a criterion may be two errorless repetitions of a list in a verbal-learning task or two negotiations of a maze without a wrong turn. Most of these data, therefore, relate primarily to the first or to the first and second phases of skill learning, but not to the final phase. This is in some respects unfortunate, because it has led many students to speak of the "asymptote," or limit, of the learning curve, as if improvement with practice actually ceased after a relatively few trials. Behavior changes may approach a limit with respect to some defined criterion but improvement is usually continuous, and any asymptote or number of trials at which learning ceases is purely arbitrary.

While the evidence is clear that subjects show continuous improvements in performance, as measured by speed, over many hundreds of trials, the underlying basis of this improvement is not clear. Some psychologists hold the view that this slow incremental development is basic to the learning process. Others argue that the basic associations are either fully present or fully absent. This position attempts to explain the incremental nature of the curves which have been presented as being a result of the fact that the skills being measured are constellations of many components, each learned in an all-or-none fashion. As additional components are learned, the overall skill appears to improve steadily. In the type of task which has been discussed these two views lead to about the same predictions, since skill is conceived of as containing many elements. However, where the component elements are few and can be more easily specified (Walker, 1967), the two views contrast more sharply.

OLD HABITS AND NEW SKILLS

After the first few years of life, learning an entirely new skill is rare. For the most part, new skills are built out of already existing skills. The learning of skills is therefore largely a matter of transfer of prior habits to new situations. The effects of prior habits show up in all three phases of the acquisition of new skills.

In the first stage, prior learning provides the common language by means of which the learner comes to understand the new task. This allows very rapid transfer of those aspects of previous skills most likely to help him in performing the new task. Instruction often calls forth the appropriate cognitive sets and expectancies. "Set" implies that the learner is prepared in advance for a particular event or class of events. A single name or cue can elicit a whole class of behavior which can be used in the new situation. The early stage of learning a new skill is characterized by the transfer of very general sets, modes of attack, and strategies appropriate to previously learned skills, which are also related to the new task. These general sets will contain aspects both appropriate to the new learning and inappropriate to it, and in the second stage the former are strengthened and the latter are weakened.

During the second, or associative, stage more specific stimulus-response relations are transferred to the new activity. The transfer of these relations has been widely studied. Both in language and perceptual-motor skills the degree of similarity between the old stimulus-response relationship and the new one is important. When a new skill requires a response opposite to one already learned in an identical or similar stimulus situation, the rate of learning the new skill is impaired. This impairment is called *negative transfer*. Notice that it is not the learning of an opposite response *per se* which leads to negative transfer, but it is the necessity of making an opposite response to the same or similar stimulus cues. On the other hand, when a response is called for in a situation similar to the one in which it was originally learned, *positive transfer* results. These principles can be demonstrated readily both in everyday life and in the laboratory. If you drive in a country in which traffic moves on the opposite side of the road from the side on which you are accustomed to driving, you are likely to find it difficult and confusing to reverse your previous learning; similarly, in cases where the faucets which control hot and cold water are reversed from their usual positions, months of learning are often required before their operation is smooth.

The effect of old habits upon new is remarkably persistent and continues into the final phase of skill learning, even after overt errors are eliminated. This is shown by the high correlation which usually exists between early progress and later performance. The initially more difficult task usually remains more difficult even after both tasks are well practiced. In addition, the effects of interference from previous habits may appear as actual errors when one is confronted with new demands. Even though you have "learned" to turn on the correct faucet and have made no errors for a long time, you may, under stress, revert to the older habit. Similarly, pilots who have learned the controls in one kind of cockpit and moved on to flying in another may under emergency conditions revert to old habits with serious consequences.

A number of interesting experiments illustrate the principles discussed above. These experiments involve an examination of the acquisition of skills, which either agree or conflict with previous habits.

In order to make such comparisons it is necessary to have information concerning the relative agreement of a new skill with previous learning. This is usually done by collecting ratings or preferences from the subjects to be used in the experiment or from a group of similar subjects. Consider, for example, the left half of Figure 4. In this

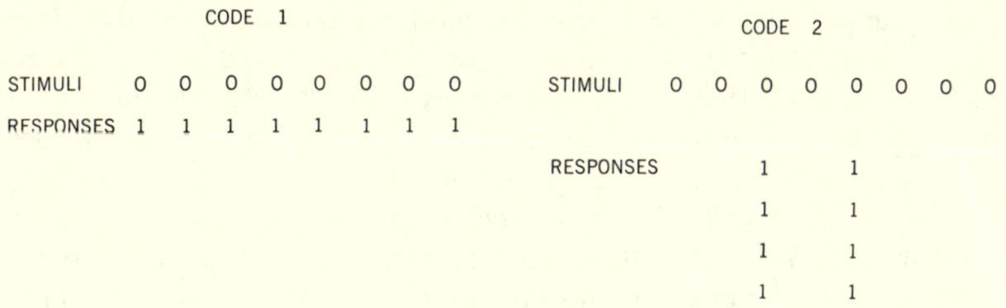

CODE 1

CODE 2

STIMULI	0	0	0	0	0	0	0	0		
RESPONSES	1	1	1	1	1	1	1	1		

STIMULI	0	0	0	0	0	0	0	0		
RESPONSES			1				1			
			1				1			
			1				1			
			1				1			

Figure 4

Two stimulus-response codes differing in level of compatability.

situation there are ten lights (stimuli) and ten keys (responses). If asked to choose which key should go with which light, virtually all subjects will assign each key to the light immediately above it. This particular arrangement, which is most in accord with previous experience, is called the *population stereotype.* If asked to choose between the arrangement shown at the left of Figure 4 and that at the right, most subjects will choose the one at the left. That is, to a set of stimuli consisting of a row of horizontal lights, the choice of a row of horizontal keys is a more popular response than is the choice of two rows of vertical keys.

Population stereotypes are now widely used in the study of both perceptual-motor and language skills. In language skills they are often called *association norms.* In both cases, however, the theoretical assumption is that the strength of old habits in individuals can be inferred from the frequency with which these habits occur in a large population of representative subjects. For example, when nearly 100 per cent of the subjects in a given population make the same choice, it is assumed that the particular association is a very strong one in each individual from that population. While the assumptions are open to dispute, experience has shown that the rate at which associations between pairs of words are learned agrees closely with predictions from association norms. The same is true for perceptual-motor skills. Here again early learning difficulties seem to persist throughout all phases of skill learning.

When a number of different stimuli and responses occur within a given task, their specific arrangements are called *stimulus codes and response codes.* For example, stimuli may be coded in terms of digits, light flashes, vibrations, etc. Typical response codes for man are words, finger movements, and facial expressions. It is possible to estimate the relative strength of various S-R connections by determining how much there has been of response stereotyping, such as was discussed in the last section. The more often a particular response code is chosen for a given stimulus code, the more *compatible* is the S-R code. In Figure 4, for example, the left S-R code is more compatible than the right, since the responses at the top are more often selected as natural for that stimulus code than are the responses at the bottom. Many experiments point up the importance of S-R compatibility in human performance.

Morin and Grant (1955) measured performance by reaction time for three different S-R codes. Reaction time represents the period between the onset of a stimulus and the initiation of the response. The stimuli were ten lights arranged in a horizontal row. In the direct-response condition, the key for a given light was directly under it; in the reversal condition, the spatial relations were reversed; for example, the left key was assigned to the right light and the right key to the left light; in the random condition, keys were arbitrarily assigned to lights. The results of the study showed that the reversal condition produced results only slightly less satisfactory than the direct code. Worst performance was for a random assignment of responses to lights.

Fitts and Deininger (1954) also studied the effect on reaction time of various stimulus codes and of several different ways of assigning stimuli to responses. Only one response code was employed. It involved moving a stylus about the size of a pencil in one of eight directions from a central point. The eight directions were spaced, like the spokes of a wheel, every 45 degrees around a circle. By far the fastest and most accurate responses were made to a circle of eight lights whose spatial positions corresponded to the eight directions of possible response motion. When a mirror-image reversal was imposed, so that up-down relations remained intact but left-right relations were reversed, time and error scores increased. Finally, when stimuli were assigned randomly to responses, performance dropped still further.

The Fitts and Deininger results are in agreement with those of Morin and Grant. Both studies show that when an ordered set of stimuli is used, reversal results in better performance than does a random assignment of stimuli to responses. The implication is that an incompatible S-R code, while slower than a compatible assignment, is not too difficult, provided the arrangement can be specified by some well-learned rule, such as reversal.

The studies reviewed so far varied the assignment of responses to stimuli. In another experiment (Fitts and Seeger, 1953), three different stimulus and response sets were employed. The different codes are shown in Figure 5. In the first two response sets, subjects had to move a single stylus held in the right hand; in the third set, subjects had to make simultaneous movements of both hands. Each set allowed eight possible responses, and these were assigned to the stimuli in accordance with data collected on the population stereotype for each S-R code. The results of a choice reaction-time study conducted with these codes are shown in the cells of Figure 5. Notice that no single response set is best with all stimuli. The "best" response set depends upon which stimulus set is used.

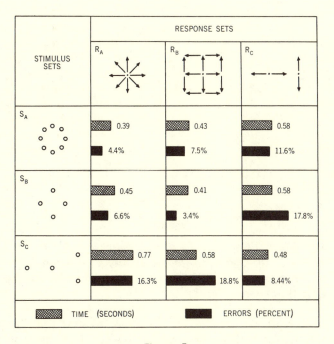

Figure 5

Error and speed data for nine different stimulus-response sets. (Adapted from Fitts and Seeger, 1953.)

The principle that performance depends upon the relation between stimulus and response sets or codes has been demonstrated in many experiments. For example, if arabic numerals are used as a stimulus, the fastest response results from the use of their names; if lights are used as stimuli, a key press is much faster than naming.

It makes no sense to ask what response code is best for man, because the question has no general answer but depends upon the particular stimulus arrangement.

Fitts and Seeger (1953) carried out the training for some of their conditions for twenty five sessions spaced over three months. The results for one high- and one low-compatibility condition are shown in Figure 6. The figure is plotted on logarithmic axes and both conditions

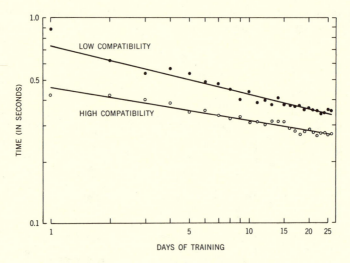

Figure 6

Gradual improvement, with practice, in tasks involving high- and low-compatibility stimulus-response codes. (Adapted from Fitts and Seeger, 1953.)

show the typical linear improvement over the full training period. However, even with this level of training, the condition which was most compatible at first remained significantly faster in the end. The results indicate the persistence of these compatibility relations. They extend into the final phase of skill learning. There is a slight tendency for the low-compatibility condition to show a steeper slope, but it is doubtful that it would catch up with the high compatibility condition after any reasonable training period.

Several important conclusions can be summarized. First, performance depends both upon the stimulus and the response codes. A particular response code may lead to improved performance with one stimulus code and not with another. Second, performance as measured by speed and number of errors is usually in agreement with the degree of compatibility of the S-R code obtained from population stereotypes. Third, the effects of compatibility will continue over long periods of practice if performance is assessed by speed or ability to perform the task together with another task. Finally, the source of compatibility effects may lie in previous learning or in the basic structure of the human nervous or muscular system. In most cases genetic and learned factors both are probably involved.

OTHER ASPECTS OF LEARNING

In this chapter no attempt has been made to deal systematically with the entire field of learning. Instead, emphasis has been on a few topics which are often neglected but which are especially important for an understanding of human performance in complex tasks. These include the hierarchical and sequential organization of skills, the long-continued duration of skill learning, and the continuing reorganization of new skills out of old ones. Modern learning theory has often dealt with simpler processes than these. Thus Donald Hebb, in his 1960 presidential address before the American Psychological Association entitled "The American Revolution," credited the past fifty years with the achievement of a rigorous understanding of many simpler learning processes within the framework of S-R theory, but at the same time urged American psychologists to get on with the analysis of more complex processes. The thesis of this book is that skills vary in complexity. The study of skilled performance must cover the complete spectrum from very simple to very complex processes, including the use of language. It is hoped that this analysis of skill will give insight into the abilities which man brings to complex tasks.

The treatment of motivation and performance will be briefer than the preceding discussion of learning and performance. It is necessary to deal with motivation for many of the same reasons it was necessary to deal with learning. Performance is always determined by the level of motivation as well as by the extent of learning. The term "motivation" is used here in a broad sense. It refers to activity level, alertness, fatigue, and other factors besides learning which determine human output at any moment. Most treatments of motivation are principally concerned with instincts and with primary drives such as hunger, which play a relatively small role in the topics discussed in this volume. Accordingly, as was the case with learning, only selected aspects of motivation—those which are crucial to skills—will be considered.

POTENTIAL VERSUS ACTUAL PERFORMANCE

Many machines are designed to operate at a fixed rate. A computer may have a fixed cycle time, memory capacity, and limit as to the length of the words it can store. Radar may utilize a fixed antenna-rotation and pulse-repetition rate. It is relatively easy to compute the capacity of such systems. Man is different. Not only does his capacity vary with learning and with each of thousands of different tasks, but it varies also as a function of a variety of other factors which fall under the heading of motivation. This, of course, makes the task of predicting human performance a great deal more difficult. One must take into account learning and motivation, as well as task variables, as determinants of performance level.

One revealing way of viewing the relation of motivation to performance has been proposed by Helson (1964) in his *hypothesis of par or tolerance*. Stated simply, the hypothesis is that in most tasks individuals set for themselves some standard of excellence and are content to meet but do not strive to exceed this standard. This adaptation or aspiration level is habitually set below the level of performance they actually are capable of achieving.

The hypothesis of par is part of a pervasive tendency for scales of subjective judgment to show a neutral point or adaptation level. The neutral point for judging the intensity of a stimulus depends upon previous experience with other stimuli of a similar type, and upon the present background. In the same way, the level of acceptable performance depends upon the subjects' previous successes and failures within this and related contexts, and upon the present stimulus situation.

Unfortunately, it is not always possible to specify how the occurrence of success or failure in a task will affect the subject's aspirations concerning future performance. The most widely accepted generalization from experiments concerning this issue (Cofer and Appley, 1964) is that successful performance leads to an increase in the standard of excellence, while failure leads to a decrease. There can be exceptions— for example, when long-continued success leads to boredom with a task and an unwillingness to expend additional effort.

Many experiments show that the level of performance can be varied by arranging the task to suggest that a high level of performance is expected. For example, Mace (1953) improved performance in an aiming task simply by adding more concentric rings, within the established periphery, thus making what previously appeared to be good performance look mediocre. The experimenter may also vary performance by manipulating the instructions to indicate that good scores have been obtained by others.

Evidence that performance rarely lives up to the potential of the subject is obtained by an analysis of the relation between subjective reports and actual performance levels under stress. Temperature and humidity, for example, do have some effect on performance of certain tasks, but this occurs at a point well beyond that at which subjects begin to complain strenuously about discomfort. Left to his own devices, man will often stop work before he has to. In this situation, too, an effort by the experimenter to supply the subject with relevant standards obtained in similar situations will vary the performance.

The preceding analysis suggests that individuals may work closer to their capacities when they are provided with objective criteria of their performance relative to their own previous performance and that of others. In the next section the role of such information in governing the level of performance will be considered.

FEEDBACK

Much of the incentive which motivates the activities of man comes from the consequences of his own movement. If behavior is goal directed, then the successful approach to the goal can serve to sustain behavior. In order to follow current usage in cybernetics, control theory, and much of psychology, we shall call information arising as a consequence of the organism's response "feedback." It is possible to consider two

types of feedback. The first, *intrinsic feedback,* is a natural consequence of the movement itself. When you move your hand, information
arising from the muscles and joints of the hand provides kinesthetic
cues about its rate of movement and location. At the same time,
information from the eyes and perhaps other sources as well arises
as a consequence of the motion. This kind of feedback arises naturally
from any response of the organism and is not dependent on external
or artificial cues from the environment. The second type of feedback
is called *augmented feedback*; it is extrinsic to the organism. Suppose,
for example, that as your hand moves, the experimenter announces
when it is coming closer to the goal. Here an external source is
providing feedback about the consequences of the movement.

Feedback, either intrinsic or augmented, may serve three functions. It can provide *knowledge, motivation,* and *reinforcement.* The
first of these functions has been mentioned above. Feedback can be
processed just like information resulting from any other stimulus. It
may also serve as a reward, providing extremely strong motivation to
continue a task, since it relates to the distance between a present
state and a goal. Since feedback operates as a strong source of motivation, it may be an important or even a necessary condition for learning.
A reinforcer is a stimulus the occurrence of which serves to strengthen
responses in close temporal proximity to it. In this sense, feedback,
both intrinsic and augmented, serves as a powerful reinforcer in the
learning of skills. Whether all knowledge provided by feedback, or only
its rewarding aspects, provides the basis for its reinforcing properties
is ·not fully known. In the next two sections some important experiments will be discussed that illustrate the role of feedback in the
development of skills.

INTRINSIC FEEDBACK

In normal situations, intrinsic feedback is always with us. However, in some industrial contexts, and more often in the experimental
laboratory, information from the natural consequences of our movements can be interrupted or distorted. The use of artificial limbs is
a familiar instance of reduced feedback: information from muscles and
joints is eliminated and manipulation must depend mainly upon visual cues. When walking on stilts one has something of this problem
since these artificial appendages do not provide the proprioceptive information which normally accompanies leg movements. Here again visual
cues can be used to compensate to some degree for kinesthetic
deficit.

In the laboratory it is much easier to interrupt, delay, or distort
feedback which is processed through visual or auditory channels than

that which arises from the muscles or joints. Such work began in the early history of experimental psychology; an example is the classical studies of Stratton (1897), who wore prisms which inverted the visual world. He reported that over time he learned to adapt to the distortion so that his performance became close to normal. Recent studies have shown that performance in tasks that involve inversions and reversals of the visual field can be improved over time in much the same way as performance in tasks that involve low-compatibility codes can be improved. For example, in a book devoted to such experiments, Smith and Smith (1962) report one study which investigated tracing a star. In it, direct visual feedback from the hand was eliminated and the subject viewed his performance in a television monitor. The star was shown either directly, reversed, inverted, or both reversed and inverted. Performance was studied for twelve trials distributed over four days. The results for three conditions are shown in Figure 7. The

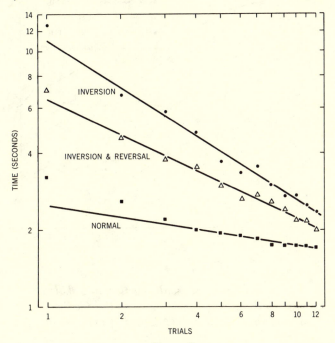

Figure 7

Gradual improvement, with practice, in tasks with differing feedback. (Adapted from K. U. Smith and W. M. Smith, Perception and Motion. *Philadelphia: W. B. Saunders Company, 1962. Reprinted with permission.)*

subjects seem to be improving in the distorted conditions much as if they were learning a new perceptual-motor skill. The differences between conditions, however, maintain themselves out to the longest practice period studied.

Even when the sources of feedback are eliminated, performance can often adjust readily to their absence. The use of intense noise to prevent a subject from hearing his own voice does not disrupt his speech unduly, though it may cause him to speak louder. In a recent study, Gould (1965) had subjects transfer pins from one hole to another

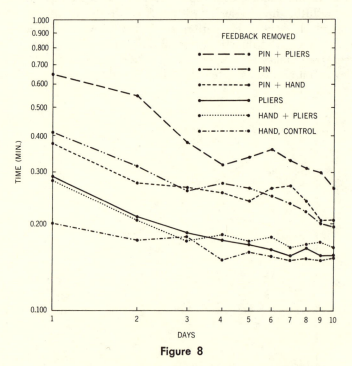

Figure 8

Gradual improvement, with practice, in a skilled task with varying components of the feedback information removed. (Adapted from Gould, 1965.)

with a small pliers. The subjects observed their performance on a television monitor which permitted the experimenter to eliminate the subject's view of the pins, the pliers, his own hand, or any combination of pins, pliers, and hand. Figure 8 shows the mean time required to transfer the pins with various sources of feedback removed. Notice that the elimination of the target (pins) caused the most disruption. However, improvement was made under all conditions. These studies indicate that performance can be maintained in the absence of much of the usual feedback. None of the studies, however, eliminated all sources of feedback. In the study cited above, even when all *visual* information was eliminated, the subject still had considerable kinesthetic feedback. In the same way, noise may prevent the subject from hearing his own speech, but it does not eliminate vibration through the head bones, nor information from the muscles of the speech system. It is virtually impossible to eliminate all sources of feedback in studies of the intact human being. But in spite of the inability to eliminate all sources of feedback these studies suggest the following: eliminating or distorting any component of the feedback will disrupt performance; practice under the new feedback conditions leads to improvement; and the performance of a group with disrupted feedback catches up only slowly, if ever, with a control group having normal feedback.

More serious decrements in performance occur when feedback is delayed and then presented to the subject within the same serial task. Earlier (page 3), it was suggested that playing back to a subject his own voice with delays below one second makes speech difficult or impossible. Much the same is true if feedback is delayed in other skilled activities, such as sending Morse code. Adjustment of performance to delayed feedback is particularly difficult.

In summary, the distortion of normal intrinsic feedback has considerable disruptive effect upon performance. In many cases, adjustment can be made through learning, but adjustment to a condition of reduced or distorted feedback is much like learning an entirely new skill and only slowly, if at all, does the activity reach the automated stage which would apply under conditions of normal feedback.

AUGMENTED FEEDBACK

It is also possible to increase the level of feedback by providing external sources of information. In one laboratory experiment on pattern recognition it was discovered, by accident, that the use of noisy counters, which clicked off the seconds, greatly improved performance over what it had been when quiet clocks were used, even though subjects in both conditions were told their time score after each trial. Having the counters present apparently served to increase the subjects' motivation.

Alfred Smode (1958) studied this effect systematically, using a tracking task in which two groups of subjects learned to keep centered a randomly varying needle by rotating a dial. For two sessions, one group was given normal feedback in the form of a verbal report, after each trial, of the length of time the needle had been on target (centered). The other group was given augmented feedback by means of a counter on which their score was accumulated. The very striking results are shown in Figure 9. Notice that from the first trial the

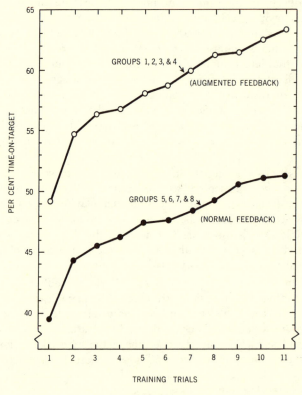

Figure 9

Practice curves for tracking tasks with and without augmented feedback. (After Smode, 1958.)

group receiving augmented feedback shows much higher performance.

The fact that the performance of the "augmented" group was better from the first trial suggests that the effect of the additional feedback was to motivate the subject to work harder during each trial. An important theoretical and practical question is whether the augmented group, working at a higher level of motivation, also learns more. Will the higher level of performance in the augmented group be likely to endure and will the contrast persist when the two groups are working under similar conditions? In order to determine the answers to these questions, Smode brought his subjects back on a second day and had one half of each group work under the feedback conditions of the other group and the other half remain with the conditions they had been using. The groups which had received augmented feedback the first day showed better performance than the other groups whether or not they continued to receive the additional feedback.

In summary, motivation can be improved through the use of augmented feedback. This improvement is reflected in increased performance not only when the added feedback is present, but also when conditions are returned to normal. These results have important implications for establishing the proper conditions for training skills.

PERFORMANCE AND STRESS

We shall define "stress" not as a condition that feels stressful to the individual, but by a specification of the demands that the environment places on the individual. Defined in this way, stress has the same meaning in testing man as it does in testing materials and machines. Stress on a system is varied by changing the load, temperature, vibrations, etc. The advantage of so defining stress is that it makes of it an independent variable. The definition leaves open the empirical question of what effect these variables have on human performance, and if we like, on the subjective feelings of stressfulness, boredom, challenge, etc.

When stress is defined by the demands a task makes, it is immediately apparent that people do their best under intermediate conditions of stress. Remove all input—all environmental variation, all demands—and the individual at best becomes bored, loses alertness, and perhaps goes to sleep. At worst, he exhibits some of the hallucinations and cognitive deficit sometimes reported in experiments specifically designed to study sensory deprivation. People also do poorly at the other extreme of stress. Increase the task load to the point where it is impossible for the individual to keep up with the demands placed upon him, or change the environmental conditions until they approach the limits of tolerance for temperature, humidity, vibration, illumination, pressure, or noxious gases, and performance again deteriorates. Man's best performance and the conditions of work that he reports as most challenging, stimulating, and conducive to maximum effort, are found in between such extremes. Three specific topics relating to stress will be considered: first, the way an individual adapts to input overload, or task stress; second, the way he responds to environmental stress; and finally, the condition of stress that he prefers or finds most conducive to successful effort.

INFORMATION OVERLOAD

James G. Miller (1964) has written extensively about the mechanisms whereby the individual adjusts to conditions in which the rate of incoming signals is beyond his capacity. The following discussion is based in large part on Miller's analysis. One way of responding to input overload is to work faster and faster and *let errors increase;* in other words, make less carefully considered decisions and respond without considering all the information. Man can vary the rate at which he works. If he attempts to work too fast, his errors are likely to increase. In most instances, letting errors increase is not an efficient way to handle information input overload.

Another of man's mechanisms for adapting to input overload is to *disregard or filter out part of the information.* It may seem as though letting this mechanism function is like letting errors accumulate, since omissions are often equivalent to errors. However, filtering or omitting may be selective. Wherever there is some basis for establishing priorities, and provided there is some readily available cue or tag that identifies the less important information, filtering may permit the individual to do a relatively effective job. He handles important messages or decisions and simply puts the remainder aside. Students do this when an important examination is coming up the next morning. So do men in important decision-making positions who often delegate less important decisions to subordinate levels in the organizational hierarchy.

A third mechanism is *queuing.* Here, input messages and other work are simply allowed to wait in line. Such waiting lines delay the output relative to the input. In some tasks, a delay is equivalent to an error, though in others it has definite advantages. It permits the irregularities in input to be smoothed out and irregularly spaced input to be turned into a uniformly spaced flow of work. The scheduling of work in a manufacturing plant, the transportation of supplies, the distribution of mail, even the use of the time of a physician during open office hours can be made more efficient from the point of view of the worker (but not necessarily from that of the customer) by employing a waiting line. In most complex human performance a waiting line, in the form of short-term or buffer memory, is almost a necessity. We would find it impossible to understand human speech if we had to respond instantaneously to each phoneme, syllable, or word. To understand speech we must examine longer strings of words. In order to read, play music, type, or drive a car effectively, the eye must take in information considerably in advance of the vocal or manual output. More will be said later about these phenomena in human performance. At this point it will be sufficient simply to note that man's ability to cope effectively with patterned input, and to organize his own patterned output, is in large measure dependent on his ability to accumulate a small amount of information before beginning to respond to it.

A few other mechanisms of adjustment to information overload have been proposed by Miller and by others. At the most extreme, an individual may simply stop work for a time. This may sound like highly nonadaptive behavior, but in some situations it is desirable. For example, sometimes it is better for the pilot to take his hands off the controls and depend on the built-in stability of the aircraft than for the pilot to try to return the plane to level flight. Pilots also learn not to fight certain types of atmospheric turbulence but to depend on the statistical likelihood that downdrafts and updrafts will average out.

ENVIRONMENTAL STRESS

In the last section, we considered stress due to environmental signals or information relevant to a particular task. Stress may also occur from energy or information which is irrelevant to the requirements of an assigned task. Environmental stress may arise from many different sources, but there will be space here to consider only two general aspects of the relation between stress and performance.

The first generalization about stress is an obvious one; high levels of stress tend to reduce efficiency. It is proper, however, to realize the extent of man's tolerance for stress as well as his limitations. Man can adapt to a wide range of environmental changes. This is particularly true for his sense organs. The eye can read and recognize patterns over changes of more than a hundredfold in illumination. The ear can take in 100 decibels of extraneous noise while the man continues to perform efficiently. Man is limited in his ability to adapt to different temperatures, but in comparison to electronic computers he has enormous tolerance for heat, cold, humidity and other changes in the environment. The source of this wide tolerance is in the homeostatic physiological mechanisms which stabilize man's internal state as his external world changes. These mechanisms are discussed in detail in another volume of this series (Butter, pending).

But stresses beyond man's tolerance for them usually result in changes in performance. Usually, subjective feelings of discomfort will anticipate actual changes in performance, but this is not always the case. Changes in performance are magnified when the irrelevant information closely resembles the relevant information. Thus small amounts of extraneous conversation will cause larger changes in performance in tasks involving the use of words than will much more intense noise of a nonverbal kind.

The second fact about stress is that different sources of stress are not necessarily additive in their effect. When stresses from two sources are combined, the relative effects upon performance may be the sum of the two, greater than the sum, or even less than either stress alone. Sometimes stresses interact to cause a greater overall effect than one would predict from adding their individual effects. Crook (*et al*, 1950) found that neither vibration nor low illumination by itself had much effect upon reading performance, but when the two stresses were combined, performance deteriorated greatly. These results indicate that some stresses interact so that man is less able to deal with them together than separately. In the case of vibration and illumination this result makes sense. Reducing the illumination apparently made precise focusing of the eyes more important, but vibration interfered with the subjects' ability to focus.

On the other hand, stresses may combine to have a smaller effect upon performance than either stress alone has. Broadbent (1963b) reviewed studies which combined lack of sleep with high levels of environmental noise. Each of these stresses had adverse effects on simple search tasks, but when they were combined their effect was reduced. Again, an obvious explanation suggests itself. The usual effect of the loss of sleep is a low level of arousal. This increases the likelihood of missing information. One effect of noise is to increase the level of arousal, and thus compensate for the loss of sleep.

Both experiments and intuition suggest that stresses combine in complex ways and that stress is not to be considered a single thing.

OPTIMAL STRESS

Readers who continue to think of stress as something undesirable may feel that the expression "optimal stress" is a contradictory one. What it implies is that there are some levels of irrelevant stimulation and of relevant information that are either preferred by the individual or conducive to the best performance or both. As was pointed out earlier, the agreement between preference and output may not be exact.

Because of the complexity of the idea of stress, one must be cautious in trying to define an optimal level. The oldest formulation of this idea, the Yerkes-Dodson law, suggested that the optimal level of irrelevant stimulation increases as the level of task difficulty (relevant information) decreases. This means that for an easy task the optimal level or irrelevant stimulation will be much higher than it is for a difficult task. This idea is in accord with the common experience that repetitive tasks can often be performed best while one is listening to the radio or to an outside conversation, but that serious work involving much concentration is hampered by outside stimulation.

Most of the experimental evidence on this question has come from work with animals. The typical finding is that the optimal level of stress, as defined by the amount of deprivation of food or other bodily need, is highest for easy tasks and becomes lower the more difficult the task becomes. One explanation for this effect is that high levels of irrelevant stimulation interfere with the flexibility of behavior necessary for the solution of complex problems. Work with human subjects has tended to confirm some of these ideas. Experiments on sensory deprivation which produced very low levels of irrelevant stimulation show that this situation is not conducive to good performance, but rather can be greatly disruptive. Anxious subjects, who are characterized by chronically high levels of motivation, tend to do better than low-anxiety subjects on very simple learning tasks such as classical conditioning. The high level of their motivation apparently aids performance when the task is simple. However, they do no better and perhaps even worse, on complex learning tasks, particularly those requiring novel responses (Cofer and Appley, 1964).

These data all suggest that relevant and irrelevant stress are compensatory to some degree. That is, what is important is the total level of stimulation, both relevant and irrelevant. We have optimal performance when the total stimulation is at some intermediate level. This generalization has much to recommend it, but it must be applied with caution, especially when there are multiple sources of stimulation which may operate by different mechanisms in affecting behavior. Moreover, the effects of stress are not static, but change as the task goes on. These dynamic aspects of stress will be considered in the next section.

ALERTNESS AND FATIGUE

It is generally assumed that one loses alertness after long-continued work under low-stress conditions, while one becomes fatigued as a result of long-continued work under high-stress conditions. From the point of view developed in the last two sections, fatigue and loss of alertness have much in common. Both of them represent decrements in performance that occur over time and that increase as the stress conditions depart from the optimal level.

A typical task which results in a decrement in performance due to loss of alertness is one involving vigilance. Vigilance tasks are designed to investigate conditions in which man monitors for events which occur at rare intervals. Such tasks have become increasingly frequent in every-day life, as automatic equipment more and more regularly performs routine operations. Monitoring a radar scope, watching for defective industrial products, and adjusting deviations in the rate of water flow-ing over a dam are typical examples. It has been found almost univer-sally in laboratory studies that the probability of detecting a signal declines with the time the subject spends on the task. This decline is usually attributed to loss of alertness because of the low task require-ments.

A typical task in which fatigue is likely to result is tracking. In this task a subject must make continual adjustments as the course he is trying to follow changes from moment to moment. It is much like driving a car in traffic on a windy day when the movements of the car are not very predictable. Usually performance in such a task will show an improvement over time, as a result of continued learning. However, if the subject is already highly skilled, efficiency will decrease the longer the task is continued, and this decrease is attributable to fatigue.

Recently, Jane Mackworth (1964) compared a number of tasks resembling either the vigilance, the tracking, or the reaction-time situa-tion described previously. She used data from highly skilled subjects only, in order to minimize improvements in performance due to learn-ing. The results of a number of these studies are shown in Figure 10. The vertical axes represent measures of performance. The left-hand vertical axis is a detection index, which reflects the percentage of correct targets for the vigilance tasks. The right-hand vertical axis indi-cates the time on target for the tracking task or the time it took to begin a response for the reaction-time tasks. The horizontal axis shows the time in minutes which the subjects spent on the task during a given session. The figure shows the results of five different studies. Curves 3 and 5 indicate that the probability of detecting a correct signal in a visual vigilance task declines uniformly over time. Curve 4 shows that the percentage of time during which the subject success-fully stays on target in the tracking task also falls uniformly over the session. Curves 1 and 2 indicate that the time it takes to respond to dim, irregular lights increases with length of time spent on the task. Notice that the drop in curves 3, 4, and 5, and the rise in curves 1 and 2 both indicate that performance is declining uniformly as a function of time. This is true for both passive vigilance tasks and active tracking tasks.

Mackworth suggests that the basis for these results is the subjects' inability to give sustained attention to a single source of sensory sig-nals. Both the active and passive tasks used here require sustained

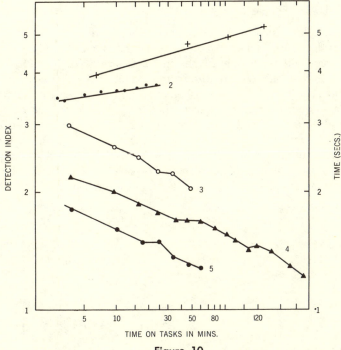

Figure 10

*Reduction in efficiency of performance as work
continues in highly overlearned perceptual-
motor skills. (Adapted from Mackworth, 1964.)*

attention because the subject never knows for sure when a signal will
arrive. If his attention shifts or his concentration lapses when a signal
occurs, his performance is reduced. Mackworth reinforced this conclusion by showing that rest pauses, knowledge of results, and drugs all
had similar effects in that they reduced performance loss on both types
of tasks.

One important mechanism by which performance is varied over
time seems to be the degree to which the subject maintains attention
upon the relevant information. Irrelevant information will have greater
effect upon performance as the time on task continues. Of course, as
suggested earlier, not all aspects of stress operate through a single mechanism.

However, the critical importance of attention in skills seems to be
well demonstrated by these data. As the book progresses, the definition
and empirical analysis of attention will be continually refined.

INDIVIDUAL DIFFERENCES

The reader may find himself concerned that the material reported in this and in future chapters refers to limitations and general capacities of man without giving any extensive treatment of individual differences. Surely one person differs from another in the level of his motivation, in his ability to sustain attention on a single task, etc. There is no question that the topics which have been discussed do show individual differences and sometimes very large ones. The data reported here often refer to groups and may not be fully typical of any individual. Considering these differences, is it possible to develop empirical laws about the limitations of man's capacities? The burden of the argument presented in this book is a cautious yes. Consider the hypo-

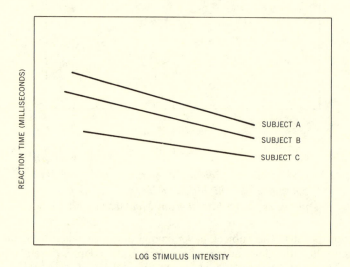

Figure 11

Hypothetical data illustrating the ability to make generalizations about some human functions despite differences between individual human subjects.

thetical data in Figure 11. In this figure, reaction time is plotted against the intensity of a stimulus. Notice that the curve for each subject is quite different with respect to the speed with which he responds. However, the independent variable, stimulus intensity, has a similar effect on every subject. That is, each subject responds more quickly to an intense than to a weak stimulus. The extent of the effect may differ but the direction and general form are similar. Thus, despite genuine differences between individuals, a general statement that reaction time decreases as intensity increases is justified. Moreover, such a general statement provides information about common aspects of human performance. Many of the general statements in this book, including those concerning the capacity for detection, memory, and recognition (see Chapter 4) are of this character. While individuals differ they are similarly affected by crucial independent variables. This book will stress the commonality among people in the effects of variables upon human performance, but it by no means denies the existence or the importance of considering differences among people.

COMPONENT PROCESSES AND
PERFORMANCE CAPACITIES

4

Scientists traditionally seek the explanation of complex phenomena in simpler ones. Experimental psychology, whose task is to provide the basic data for the analysis of human performance, operates by this logic of starting with analysis then proceeding to synthesis. The process has not been without its critics, however. Many psychologists, especially those interested in a cognitive approach to learning, perception, and problem solving, have argued that complex behavior cannot be predicted from an understanding of its elements. They further claim that efforts to analyze and study limited components of behavior have led to such simplification that the phenomena originally under investigation are no longer present.

There is much to be said for this criticism, but the crucial point to consider is the way in which skills are broken down for analysis. The best way to begin to understand skilled performance is to examine the components of behavior that are most likely to throw light on the temporally-organized patterns which constitute skills. In most of the research to be reported here, these patterns, or tasks, have been greatly simplified. The point is that skilled activities can be "taken apart" for laboratory analysis if one goes about the dissection in the right way.

The component functions selected for analysis in this chapter are those which play key roles in such complex skills as guiding a vehicle, playing chess, reading, or hitting a baseball. The data will place emphasis on those techniques in which the limits of man's capacity can be expressed quantitatively. The goal of this chapter will be to specify, as far as possible, the limits of man's ability to discriminate, recognize, time, remember, and generalize. This approach will seek to delineate human performance in terms of boundary conditions that may reflect basic human capacities.

No psychological task involves only one component function. For example, it is impossible to design a purely sensory task which does not also require some memory, attention, and response. It is possible, however, to design tasks which place primary emphasis on one or another component function. Through such tasks we obtain knowledge of various human capacities. Everyday skills can then be analyzed with respect to the load placed upon various component functions. The development of this analysis will be the goal of the next several chapters.

SENSORY CAPACITIES

The tasks to be considered in this section involve the detection, comparison, and recognition of stimuli. These functions involve more than the sense organs but have customarily been called sensory because they place emphasis upon the functions usually connected with the sense organs.

In order for a stimulus to play a role in a skill, it must be sensed by the organism. This means that it must be within the capacity of one of the human sense organs. Some lights are too dim to be seen, some tones of too high frequency to be heard, some pressures too weak to be felt. The first sensory capacity of interest then is the ability to *detect* a stimulus. A stimulus does not occur in isolation. Usually man is not attempting to detect a tone in absolute silence or a light which appears out of total darkness. There is a background of sensory stimulation out of which the stimulus in question must emerge. A stimulus then, is more properly defined as a change in the magnitude of energy impinging upon a sense organ. Thus, it is necessary to inquire into the capacity to sense a change in stimulation from any level of background present. Man's ability to make such *comparative judgments* is extremely great, as we shall see. However, when he is also required to *recognize* the stimulus, that is, to identify it from among a number of possible stimuli, he is much more limited. The three basic tasks used to measure human sensory performance, then, are detection, comparison, and recognition. We shall look briefly at each of these tasks.

DETECTION

The simplest way to conceive of a capacity for detection of stimuli would be to determine the degree of physical intensity above which the subject always reports having experienced the stimulus and below which he never reports having experienced it. Such a limit is a *fixed threshold*, but unfortunately, even the earliest experiments in detection of stimuli showed that no such fixed point can be found. Rather, a smooth curve, such as the one described in Figure 12, relates the probability of detecting a stimulus to its physical intensity. This function is known to vary not only with the type of stimulus, but also with the level of the subject's motivation, the quality of the instruction he receives, and other variables.

The fact that there is no fixed threshold leaves us with two other ways of trying to describe the limits of performance in detection tasks.

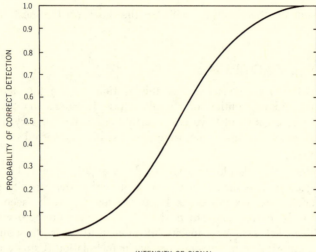

INTENSITY OF SIGNAL

Figure 12

A typical statistical threshold relating the probability of detecting a stimulus to the intensity of the stimulus. The intensity range is near the minimum which the subject can detect.

The first way is to postulate a variable or *statistical threshold* which changes from moment to moment. This view is a classical one which has much to recommend it when one is dealing with optimal sensory conditions and with highly trained subjects who are skilled at keeping constant the cues involved in their judgments. In complex tasks, however, conditions are rarely optimal. The motivation of subjects will vary depending upon how important a given signal is for the task at hand and what the competing signals are. In this situation, sensory thresholds are not nearly so important as how the subject varies the criterion for deciding if a given sensory experience constitutes a signal.

For this reason, a view of detection as a statistical process of decision making is more fruitful for an analysis of skill than a view of it as a sensory threshold, either fixed or statistical. The "statistical decision" viewpoint, called the theory of signal detection, has developed largely within the last ten years (Swets, 1964) and involves differences in both theory and method from the older threshold notion.

According to signal-detection theory, every variation in physical energy at a sense organ gives rise to some change within the organism. However, every new stimulus occurs against a background of stimulation already present. The probability of detecting the new stimulus depends upon its intensity relative to the background. Neither the background (noise) nor the stimulus (signal) is constant in its effects. Rather both can be represented by distributions such as those shown in Figure 13. These curves represent the frequency of assumed internal activity of varying magnitudes for the occurrence of the background alone or for the background and the signal together. The quantity d' is a measure of the distance between the means of the two distributions. The greater the value of d' the more likely the subject is to be able to detect the presence of the signal.

Notice that as long as the two distributions overlap it is not possible for the subject always to be correct in determining whether or not a signal occurred. The theory assumes that man decides this question by adopting a criterion (β). The vertical line in Figure 13 represents one

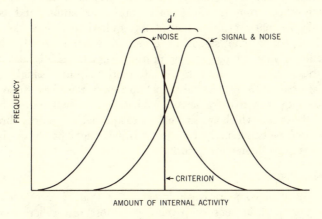

Figure 13

A hypothetical curve illustrating the theoretical distribution of varying amounts of internal activity when only noise is present and when signal-plus-noise is present. The criterion represents a point at which the subject may divide his internal activity into signal and non-signal judgments (see text).

such criterion. Any internal activity greater than the criterion will result in a report of a signal while any activity less than the criterion will result in a report of no signal. In this situation two types of errors are possible: either a signal may be missed altogether or a signal may be reported where there is none (false alarm). Notice that by shifting his criterion the subject may vary the proportion of these two types of errors, although he cannot eliminate error entirely. Suppose, for example, that a lookout is trying to spot forest fires. It might be a good strategy for him to set his criterion far to the left and report a large number of false alarms but lessen the chance of a fire starting without being detected. Or he might set it far to the right, minimizing the number of false alarms but increasing the possibility of undetected fires. Clearly, his instructions, including the rewards for being correct and the punishments for error can be thought of as causing variation in the criterion which he uses.

While there is continuing dispute about the relative advantages of the threshold and the signal-detection viewpoints in sensory psychology, there can be no question about the value of the latter for discussing limitations in skilled performance. The reason is that it allows for computation of a sensory capacity (d'). The effects of this capacity may be distinguished from those of instruction, motivation, and competing signals. In many tasks, a person is required to reduce the probability of detecting one signal in order to enhance the probability of detecting a more important, or priority, signal. Man is also limited in his ability to select, over time, information from a single sensory source (see pages 37–39). Signal detection theory can place these limitations into a quantitative framework. What follows, will rarely be concerned with stimuli which are so weak as to approach a sensory threshold, but will often be concerned with signals which might be missed because man has assigned them a low priority.

COMPARISON

The study of comparative judgment, like that of thresholds, plays an important part in sensory psychology. Most researchers interested in sensory modalities study comparative judgment. For example, they will present two stimuli (standard and test) and require the subject to judge them to be the same or different, indicate which of the two is more intense, or adjust one (the test stimulus) until it equals the other (the standard stimulus). People are very good at making such judgments, especially if they are not hurried. For example, under good viewing conditions a typical subject can detect a difference of as little as 2 per cent in the brightness of two adjacent fields, and over a considerable range of stimulus frequencies the ear can reliably detect a change of less than 6 cycles per second.

The amount of stimulus change which can be detected is approximately proportional to the size or intensity of the standard. That is, the subject is able to detect changes of a fixed percentage of the standard stimulus. This generalization is called *Weber's Law*, after the German physiologist who first formulated it. Details about the capacity for comparative judgment for different sensory modalities are discussed elsewhere in this series (Alpern, Lawrence, and Wolsk, 1967). Like the question of sensory threshold, however, the capacity for comparison is not central in the analysis of skills. Skills are usually performed under the stress of time or at least with some premium paid on rapid as well as accurate performance. Besides, in most skilled tasks there is no standard against which to compare each stimulus. The question is usually how to classify a given stimulus and not whether it is the same or different from some standard stimulus. For this reason, it is necessary to turn to data regarding the recognition and classification of sensory stimuli.

RECOGNITION

This section is concerned with man's ability to place a familiar stimulus such as a tone or color into its proper category—for example, calling a yellow color yellow, a red color red, a blue, blue, etc. This type of task is called absolute judgment. Although absolute judgments are made within the context of other events, they are unlike comparative judgments in that no explicit standard is allowed. The standards are implicit, that is, they are a part of the memory store. Thus absolute judgment is not a strictly sensory task. It tells us relatively little about the basic characteristics of individual sense organs, but a great deal about the relation of sensation to memory.

In an experiment involving absolute judgment, the experimenter selects stimuli which lie along a single sensory dimension or which possess a single quality such as pitch, loudness, lineal distance, or saltiness (see Table 1). First the experimenter familiarizes the subject with each of the stimuli he is going to use. The stimuli may, for example, consist of tones separated by 100-cycle intervals and ranging from 100 cycles per second to 5,000 cycles per second. Responses are assigned in the form of numbers in serial order: for example, the response to the lowest tone would be 1; the response to the next lowest, 2; and so on. The tones must be spaced so that any adjacent pair would be easily discriminated in a test of comparative judgment. After the subject has become completely familiar with the stimuli, and with the responses appropriate to them, the experimenter, using as a rule only two or three different stimuli to begin with, presents the stimuli in random order. The subject is required to identify them, with the appropriate responses. Gradually the number of tones to be identified is increased—perhaps even to twenty or more.

The data from such an experiment are summarized in the form of a chart, *a stimulus-response matrix*, the different stimuli being represented in the columns and the different responses in the rows (see page

89). The numbers in the cells represent the number of times the correct response was given to the stimulus represented by that column. From the chart the experimenter calculates the amount of information the subject has transmitted by his responses. In an absolute judgment experiment, the amount of information the subject transmits represents roughly the total number of stimuli the subject can recognize without error. If more than this number of stimuli are used, the subject will always make more errors. The exact method of calculating the amount of information transmitted will be explained in Chapter 5.

The results of various experiments using this technique are strikingly similar. As the experimenter increases the number of stimuli, the amount of information transmitted by the subject at first increases and then remains constant. This maximum level represents the total number of stimuli the subject can identify without error. Most subjects can identify a maximum of six tones without error. The limit or maximum capacity varies with different stimuli and different subjects, but the variations are slight. Column 4 of Table 1 shows that the maximum number of different stimuli which can be correctly identified by different subjects varies only from four to ten. Both the low limit of performance in this task and the similarity of results for different sensory qualities illustrate that absolute judgment is limited by something other than the sensitivity of the sense organs.

A typical subject is able, by *comparative* judgment, to discriminate tones that differ by as little as 3-4 cycles in the center of the frequency range. This means that within the limits of hearing the subject is able to discriminate hundreds of tones by using comparative judgment. Yet when Irwin Pollack (1952) required subjects to identify, by absolute judgment, tones ranging from 100 to 8000 cycles he found that his best subject could correctly identify only six stimuli. Furthermore, whether the range of tones used was 250 cycles or 8,000, there was little difference in the rate of error. If subjects had been able to perform at a level even approximating that of comparative judgment, they would have been able to identify hundreds of tones correctly.

An idea of individual differences can be gotten from data on absolute judgment of color obtained by Conover (1959). He found his subjects able to identify, on the average, nine colors; the range was from five to twenty-two stimuli. There was no significant difference between a population of college students and one whose job involved mixing paints in their ability to identify colors. Working with auditory tones, Pollack (1952) reported small variability due either to differences between individuals or to gross changes in the range and spacing of tones. It is true that the phenomenon of absolute pitch seems to have some experimental verification. Attneave (1959), for example, cites a concertmaster who could identify from forty to fifty different pitches. But while a few people have extraordinary ability along certain dimen-

Table 1

Capacity for Absolute Judgment Along a Single Dimension[1]

MODALITY	DIMENSION	MAXIMUM INFORMATION TRANSMITTED (BITS)[2]	APPROXIMATE NUMBER OF STIMULI CORRECTLY IDENTIFIED
Vision	Position on a line	3.3	10
Vision	Hue	3.1	9
Audition	Pitch	2.5	6
Audition	Loudness	2.3	5
Taste	Saltiness	1.9	4

[1]Data taken from Attneave (1959).
[2]This measure is explained in detail in Chapter 5.

sions, efforts to improve normal subjects through practice on absolute judgment have been only moderately successful. Hartman (1954), for example, found improvement from three to only seven correctly identified stimuli among subjects who practiced absolute judgment of tones for a period of over seven weeks. These experiments demonstrate the severe limitations in man's ability to recognize stimuli varying along a single dimension or sensory quality.

The limit on man's capacity for absolute judgment certainly rests in part on memory, since the main difference between the task of comparative judgment and that of absolute judgment is the presence of the standard in the former and its absence in the latter case. As one might expect, the addition of any kind of reference or "anchor point" improves one's capacity to make absolute judgments. In judging the position of a point along a line, for example, a subject uses the ends of the line as convenient references, and the usual capacity is somewhat better (10 correct stimuli) for this task than for tasks involving pitch or loudness or the lengths of lines where no anchor points are available. It is not possible for subjects to read scales and other instruments to an accuracy of much more than one-fifth of an unmarked interval. Instead, the required precision is achieved by the use of numbered and unnumbered scale marks, grid lines, and the like.

If people are so limited in their capacity for categorizing stimuli, then how are they able to accomplish the myriad tasks of everyday life, in which they identify faces, spoken words, printed symbols, and gestures, and read all kinds of instruments with great precision? The answer lies primarily in that they use complex, multidimensional signals. The thirty-two phonemes that make up spoken English, for example, vary from one another in intensity, duration, and frequency. The written alphabet of English also consists of complex patterns. To construct a set of legible characters out of dots, as is done in many electrical signs and scoreboards, one would need a 5 x 7 matrix or 35 yes-no elements as a minimum. One might construct a rudimentary alphabet by using as few as seven or eight lines but would need twelve to sixteen for moderately good legibility.

Investigators have studied man's capacity for making absolute judgments simultaneously along two or more dimensions. Performance is almost always less than what it would be if they were independently combining information taken from the different dimensions. The result of a study by Klemmer and Frick (1953) is typical: their subjects were able to identify without error about six positions along a line. When the task became one of locating a dot in a square, the investigators found the subjects were able to identify 23 stimuli instead of the 6 x 6 or 36 stimuli which might have been expected if the two dimensions had been judged independently and then combined. This general principle appears to apply to all multidimensional judgments. For example, Pollack and Ficks (1954) had subjects judge six different dimensions of a number of tones and found the number of stimuli which could be recognized rose to over two hundred.

In summary, man is severely limited in his ability to recognize stimuli along a single dimension: he can recognize five to ten stimuli without error. While a few individuals may have considerably greater capacity along some dimensions, the limits are only slightly changed by training. The limitation appears to be due to the inexactness of memory for a standard against which to compare each stimulus. As the number of dimensions in the stimulus is increased, the number of stimuli which can be recognized rises. However, each new dimension increases the number by fewer than would be expected if the dimensions were independent. Laboratory studies using six dimensions have succeeded in obtaining recognition of several hundred tones.

PERCEPTUAL PROCESSES

The previous section was concerned with man's ability to detect and identify stimulus change. In this section, processes of greater complexity will be considered. These processes are often called perceptual because they require higher levels of processing than are involved in the tasks of detection and identification discussed previously. Perceptual tasks investigate man's ability to select certain aspects of the stimulus situation or to detect similarities between different stimulus patterns.

PATTERN RECOGNITION

One of the most remarkable features of human information processing is the capacity to respond to patterns and relationships irrespective of the magnitude of the stimuli. A printer can vary the size of type composing a page and produce little effect on the speed or accuracy with which the page is read. We can view the printed page, the face of a friend, or any familiar object from various distances and yet respond to its constant size. The ability to recognize spoken words is even more remarkable. Within limits, a speaker can vary his rate of speech or his loudness; or another voice, with very different frequency characteristics, can take over, and the listener will continue to understand. The speaker can also use a variety of dialects with a good chance of being understood.

Scientists do not understand these phenomena well enough to build machines that have comparable flexibility. Machines cannot yet be made, for example, that can discriminate the handwriting or the speech of different people, although they can recognize printed symbols.

Some experiments have been performed which tell us about the human capacity to recognize patterns which have undergone distortion. One of the simplest ways to distort a pattern is to mix it with noise. Miller, Heise, and Lichten (1951) showed that the ability of subjects to recognize familiar words against a background of white noise (static) improved as the intensity of the word was increased with respect to the noise (signal to noise ratio). Figure 14 illustrates this effect. The curves represent words selected from populations of varying size. For example, in the top curve one of only two alternative words occurs on each trial while in the curve labelled 256 the word to be presented on a given trial is selected from 256 different words. When the number of alternatives from which the given word selected is small, then the effect of adding noise is also relatively small, and as the number of alternatives increases the noise becomes more effective. This illustrates that if an event is highly probable it will be recognized despite considerable distortion, while if the event is not very probable distortion will greatly affect recognition. The ability of man to use prior information to resist distortion can improve performance or it can harm it. Knowing the content of a radio or TV program can help you follow it despite distortion. On the other hand, in proofreading we may fail to detect an error (distortion) because the context leads us to expect and thus, in spite of the distortion, to *see* the correct pattern.

Figure 15 illustrates another kind of distortion, or noise, introduced to distort the digit 4. The level of distortion is varied by allowing the dots which make up the pattern to move varying distances from their original positions. The accuracy with which such a pattern can be

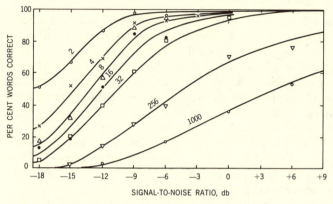

Figure 14

Percentage of correctly detected English mono-syllables as a function of the amount of noise (signal-to-noise ratio) with which the syllable is mixed. The curves represent different size populations of items varying from 2 through 1000. (After Miller, Heise, and Lichten, 1951.)

recognized decreases as the level of distortion increases (White, 1962). The accuracy of recognition can be specified precisely for each level of distortion, provided that the subject's knowledge about what the pattern might be is kept constant. In White's study the subjects only knew that each pattern they saw was one of the digits or letters. If they had been instructed that the pattern was a digit, performance would have been better, just as it was when the population of words was restricted in the study by Miller *et al* (page 51).

These studies of the recognition of words or digits involve patterns which are highly familiar. The ability to recognize patterns is a process which itself must be learned in much the same way as other skills are learned. In order to study the development of pattern-recognition skills in the adult, nonsense patterns may be used as stimuli. This reduces the influence of prior learning. Figure 16 shows an original nonsense pattern in the upper left-hand corner. The other patterns represent five levels of distortion. A very small distortion (level 1) is shown at the upper center, while the pattern at the lower right is a complete distortion of (is unrelated to) the original.

An experiment was conducted in order to understand the effect of the level of distortion upon learning to associate an original pattern with one of its distortions (Posner, 1964). Subjects learned to associate

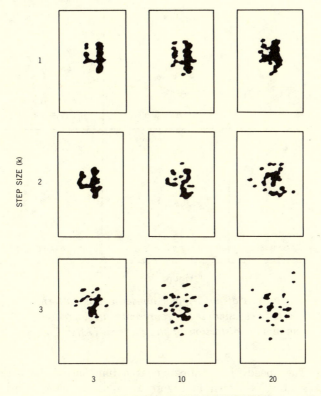

STEP SIZE (k)

NUMBER OF RANDOM WALK TRANSFORMATIONS

Figure 15

Distortions of the digit 4, composed of dots. From left to right the number of successive distortions is varied. From top to bottom the size of the step through which each dot is moved is varied. The figure illustrates the gradual loss of the ability to recognize the digit as the number and size of distortions are increased. (After White, 1962.)

six original nonsense patterns with simple names. The time to learn to associate the same names with a new list of patterns, which consisted of various levels of distortion of the originals, increased linearly with the level of distortion. Even after the subjects had learned the new list, the speed with which they could identify whether or not two patterns had been given the same name depended on the level of

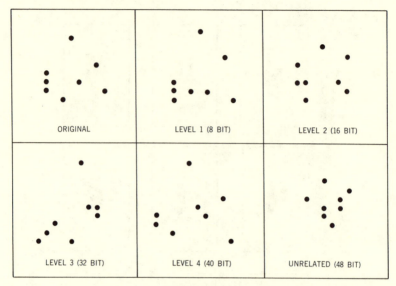

ORIGINAL   LEVEL 1 (8 BIT)   LEVEL 2 (16 BIT)

LEVEL 3 (32 BIT)   LEVEL 4 (40 BIT)   UNRELATED (48 BIT)

Figure 16

*Distortions of an original nonsense dot pattern,
Each successive level represents an increased
amount of distortion of the pattern. (After Posner, 1962.)*

distortion. The speed of classification as a function of the degree or
level of distortion is shown in Figure 17 (Posner, 1964). This study
illustrates that pattern recognition is not an effortless process, but one
which requires extensive learning. When two different patterns are to
be given the same name, it is the degree to which they are physically similar that determines the rate at which learning takes place.
For example, only after extensive learning does the ability to recognize
a printed and hand-written letter as the same become highly automated. It takes longer to identify A and *a* as the same than it does
A and A or *a* and *a*. This occurs even after a lifetime of learning that
A and *a* have the same name.

In summary, pattern recognition is an important aspect of complex
skilled behavior. It greatly reduces the number of different stimuli
with which man must deal. Since this number is severely limited, as
the data on absolute judgment indicate, pattern recognition is necessary for skilled performance. However, the ability to recognize patterns is itself a skill which, in the initial stages, takes time to learn.
Only with extended practice does the ability to recognize patterns
become highly automated and thus serve to improve overall performance.

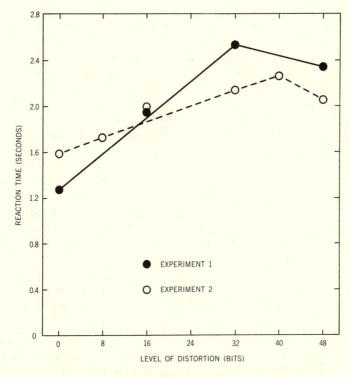

Figure 17

The time it takes to identify a pair of patterns given the same name in a prior learning experiment, as a function of the degree of distortion between the patterns. Low levels of distortion lead to rapid identification, and the time increases linearly as the distortion increases. The curves represent two separate experiments. (After Posner, 1964.)

SELECTIVE ATTENTION

E. G. Boring, in his *History of Experimental Psychology*, describes one of the earliest experiments on selective attention. The subject was instructed to *listen* for a bell and to watch a clock with a needle sweeping over its face. He was to indicate the number the needle was pointing at when the bell sounded. Notice that the instruction directed the subject's attention to the bell. The surprising results of the study were that when the bell sounded with the needle at 5, the average report of the subjects was that the needle was at 4. How could hearing the bell take place before it actually rang? This curious phenomenon led to the notion of temporal relativity in processing sensory information and was called the doctrine of prior entry, which may be summarized as follows: Man is limited in his ability to attend to signals coming simultaneously from more than one sensory source. If signals arise thus from two sources, the subject will process them in serial order. In the experiment described above, the subject was supposed to listen for the bell (auditory information). The auditory signal is processed first and information coming from the visual source is delayed. The subject has, for example, just processed the needle at 4 when the auditory signal arrives. The arrival of the auditory signal delays the processing of new visual information and the subject reports that the clock was where he had most recently seen it, namely at 4. If the instructions were changed to alert the subject to the needle rather than to the bell, the subject would probably report the bell's sounding at 6 rather than at 4.

While the doctrine of prior entry as described above is far too simple to account for all the facts in a situation involving a simultaneous sensory stimulation, it has the virtue of placing proper emphasis on the relative narrowness of human attention.

The limits on man's capacity to attend to and process signals coming from the environment, however, is not fixed or absolute. In Chapter 2 it was pointed out that as the learning of skills proceeds to advanced stages, performing the skill requires less and less active attention. Signals arising from a well-learned and habitual pattern such as walking will place relatively little demand upon attention, as can be demonstrated by man's ability to perform such skills while engaged in other demanding activities.

Man can process signals simultaneously if they are highly regular or predictable. The ability to process regular signals simultaneously is illustrated by the following experiment. A subject must press a key when a light goes on. The light goes on regularly one second after a warning signal is sounded. The length of time it takes for the subject to respond is measured. This procedure is then duplicated with an auditory signal (a tone) substituted for the light. In such a situation it has been found that response is faster to the tone than to the light. Now suppose the subject is told that the light and the tone will occur simultaneously one second after the warning signal. The subject's job now is to depress both keys, one with each hand. In this case the subject can react as fast to the two signals together as to either one alone. This is because he speeds up his response to the visual signal so that it corresponds with his response to the auditory signal. Since the two stimuli always occur together, only the auditory information need be considered. This rather obvious result illustrates an important point. When, because the task is highly regular or highly overlearned, there is no uncertainty about what will occur, man can respond to more than one signal without his response to one of them interfering with his response to the other.

Several experiments have been performed which explore the interference between simultaneous signals in more complex tasks. (See Chapter 6 for an account of some of them.) The general conclusion from these experiments is that as signals become less regular and predictable the ability to process two signals simultaneously systematically declines. Man's limitations in his ability to deal with simultaneous signals depends upon how uncertain or unpredictable they are.

What happens to information which cannot be attended to at a given moment? After all, man is constantly receiving signals from the thousands of sensory receptors in his eyes, ears, and skin. Many of these signals do not require the subject's attention. Some of them seem not to affect behavior at all, at least not in any overt way. Some of them may be delayed for brief periods of time while attention is given to something else, and are then processed later.

To provide a better idea of man's limitation in his ability to process simultaneous signals, a number of experiments have been carried out with subjects listening to two messages at once. It is well known that it is possible to pick one voice out of a crowd while allowing others to remain in the background. Sometimes, of course, a word from the background intrudes into the foreground. Cherry (1953, 1954) had subjects wear headsets which presented different materials to each ear. The subjects were instructed to repeat back (shadow) the story being presented to the left ear as they heard it. They were then tested on the information coming to the right ear. The findings were striking. The subjects could report almost nothing about what was coming to the right ear, not even gross shifts from English to French. Some things did get through, however. For example, the subjects often reported hearing their own name when it came to the ear they were instructed to ignore. They also reported very gross changes in acoustic pattern, such as from a voice to a musical instrument. Furthermore, when the same message being shadowed on the left ear was played into the right ear, but delayed so that it followed behind the shadowed message, subjects would spontaneously report that the right ear was now providing the same information as the shadowed ear. When the same experiment was performed with bilinguals they spontaneously reported the correspondence between messages played to the two ears even when the two messages were in different languages (Tries-man, 1965).

These experiments yield a puzzling picture of the limits of man's ability to process simultaneous messages. Although he is limited in the number of sources of sensory information he can process at one time, he can select and process messages presented to senses not being sampled at a given moment. In order for the subject to sample information being fed into the non-shadowed ear, he must somehow switch his attention to that ear.

What are the findings concerning man's limits in his ability to shift attention? Donald Broadbent (1958) reported a series of experiments concerning factors which govern such shifts. In one, a series of three digits was read into one ear and a different series was read into the other. For example, the first digit to the left ear might be 3 while the first digit to the right ear might simultaneously be 6.

After three digits were presented to each ear, the subjects were to report them back in the order in which they had been presented. When the rate of presentation was less than 1 pair per second, this was no problem, but as soon as the rate was increased subjects began to report first all the digits presented to one ear then all those presented to the other. This suggests that the subjects were unable readily to shift their attention from one ear to the other and, therefore, processed the digits from one channel prior to processing those from the other.

Subsequent experiments have shown that the ability to switch between sensory channels is a function of more than the rate at which information is presented. If a coherent sequence of information can be obtained by alternating ears the subjects seem able to shift attention even when the rate is high. Nevertheless, increases in the rate and density of information presented to one channel decreases the ability to switch between channels. No fixed or absolute switching time has been discovered.

If attention must be switched from one channel to another in order to process information, how is it possible that some items on unattended channels are reported? In both the Cherry and the Broadbent studies some information on the irrelevant channel was reported. In order for this to happen, some system must preserve the information coming to the irrelevant channel until it can be processed. In the section on memory, direct evidence for such a short term sensory storage system will be considered.

RATE OF SEARCH

One aspect of selective attention which plays an important role in skills is the ability to find and identify a pattern out of an array of stimuli. This problem involves both pattern recognition and attention, since the task is to recognize one pattern (target) and to concentrate on it, ignoring others.

If a subject is asked to look through a large number of items to find the one which has been designated the target, the relationship between the total number of items through which the subject must search and the time required to find the target item is linear. Neisser *et al.* (1963) found that when the items were letters of the alphabet the slope of this function was about 100 milliseconds per item. The slope represents the time it took to process a single item. The slope does not include the time it took to report the target but only the length of time it took subjects to consider whether or not each item was the target. The rate at which this was done improved greatly over time. Like other skills, this type of task becomes so highly automated with practice that subjects report that they do not really *see* the non-target items. The rate at which items are searched depends upon the nature both of the target item and of the surrounding population. As the target and the other items are made to resemble each other more and more it becomes increasingly difficult to find the target, and processing takes longer. If instead of looking for a single letter one has to look for a target of a given meaning, such as a proper name out of a set of other words, the time it takes to process each item becomes much greater.

Just as some skills require that we select one item out of an array simultaneously or sequentially present, others require that we select an item from memory. In fact, all recognition involves memory. When you are asked to name a letter presented to you visually, you must match the pattern you see with one that is stored and that is linked to a verbal response. How we match patterns and how the memory is stored are questions which are as yet unanswered.

It is possible to consider limitations to the rate at which memory can be searched. Chase and Posner (1965) compared rates for searching memory and for searching a visual field. In one condition (visual comparison), subjects had to find a single target letter in a visually presented array of from one to four letters. In a second condition (memory search), they memorized an array of the same size and again had to locate a single letter. The array was selected from a population of eight letters and was changed on every trial. In both conditions (visual and memory) the subject's task was to press a key as rapidly as possible to indicate whether or not the target was a member of the array. Figure 18 shows the mean reaction time as a function of the number of items in the array for both the visual task and the memory task. Notice that the functions relating the number of items searched to RT are linear, and they are virtually identical: the rate of searching through memory and searching through a physical stimulus are just about the same.

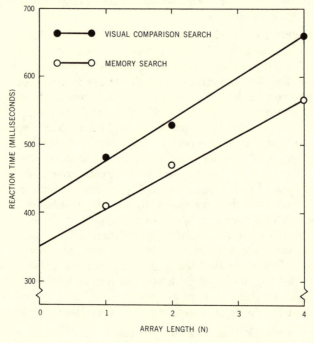

Figure 18

The time it takes to search a present stimulus array (visual comparison) and a previous stimulus (memory search) for a single target letter, as a function of the number of letters in the array. (After Chase and Posner, 1965.)

A critical aspect of searching memory is the degree to which the search can be automated under the proper conditions. In Chase's study the array was changed on every trial. Neisser *et al.* (1963) required subjects to search a visual array for one of several target sets which remained constant over trials. In different conditions the target sets consisted of one, five, or ten items.

For each trial the array contained either no target or one target, but the subjects never knew in advance which of the possible targets in the set they were using would be present. Subjects practiced for twenty-seven days. At first, the more items the subject had to look for (the larger the target set), the longer the processing took. But after twenty days' practice it took no longer to look for a target which might be any one of ten items than for a target which was always the same item. This change in the character of the search from successive to simultaneous doubtless accounts for the speed at which we are able to recognize a letter, number, or familiar word. If, every time we saw a letter, we had to search through the alphabet at the rate shown in Figure 18, skills like reading and listening would be impossible. Such rates apply only to populations which are new to the subject. Man's search among the highly familiar and overlearned sets stored in his memory tends to become increasingly simultaneous and the duration of the search does not appear to increase with the number of items through which it takes place.

MEMORY PROCESSES

The study of human memory processes has received a great deal of emphasis in recent years. Most of the findings are of direct relevance to an understanding of human capacities in skilled tasks, because even the simplest forms of skilled performance require some temporary storage of information. This section will be divided into three topics. First, there is a review of the older literature on the spans of attention and memory. Second, there is a consideration of more recent data on short-term sensory storage and short-term memory. Finally, there is an analysis of the role of memory processes in serial tasks.

SPANS OF ATTENTION AND MEMORY

The question of how many objects the mind may apprehend simultaneously arose prior to the birth of experimental psychology. According to Woodworth (1938), Sir William Hamilton, lecturing to students at the University of Edinburgh on Metaphysics and Logic in 1859, summarized the problem and its answer as follows:

> How many of several objects can the mind simultaneously survey not with vivacity, but without absolute confusion? I find this problem stated and differently answered, by different philosophers, and apparently without a knowledge of each other. By Charles Bonnet the mind is allowed to have a distinct notion of six objects at once; by Abraham Tucker the number is limited to four; while Destutt-Tracy again amplifies it to six. The opinion of the first and last of these philosophers, appears to me correct. You can easily make the experiment for yourselves, but you must beware of grouping the objects into classes. If you throw a handful of marbles on the floor, you will find it difficult to view at once more than six, or seven at most, without confusion; but if you group them into twos, or threes, or fives, you can comprehend as many groups as you can units; because the mind considers these groups only as units.

Note that Hamilton had a conception of both a limit to the number of separate items which can be grasped simultaneously (span of attention) and the importance of the role of active grouping in determining this limit.

Most experiments on the span of attention have required subjects to report the number of dots present in a 100-millisecond visual flash. Typical findings are that the attention span (number of dots reported with 50 per cent accuracy) is about eight (Woodworth, 1938). Recent studies (e.g., Averbach, 1963) have indicated that this span of attention is not fixed but depends upon the exposure time. For example, if the flash is reduced to 40 milliseconds' duration, only one item can be reported with 50 per cent accuracy. The level of accuracy increases at the rate of one item every ten milliseconds until a total of eight items is reached. Why does the span level out at eight items? Perhaps the subject experiences increasing difficulty in keeping track of which items have already been counted. This suggests that limitations in the span of attention depend upon the limits of memory.

Glanville and Dallenbach (1920) varied both the number of objects and the amount of information they asked subjects to report about each object. They showed patterns of dots and asked for the number; letters, and asked for their names; geometrical figures, and asked for the names of the figures; and figures that had to be identified by both form and color. The investigators found that the average number of objects reported with complete accuracy was as follows: number of dots, 8.8; number of letters, 6.9; number of geometrical forms, 3.8; number of forms identified by both shape and by color, 3.0. It is clear that the more information that was called for, the fewer the number of objects that were reported correctly. The reports of the subjects also indicated that their performance had depended largely upon memory. One subject, for example, said about the array of stimulus letters, "All were equally clear; could have reported all if report could have been instantaneous. Lost memory images of the last letters before I came to them."

More recently, Mackworth (1964) has demonstrated the relationship between attention span and memory. She found that the rate at which the names of digits, letters, colors, and shapes could be read out loud varied. Digits were fastest, then letters, then colors, then shapes. She then found that the number of items which could be reported from a brief exposure of the same duration for each category was greatest for digits and smallest for shapes. The faster the items could be named, the greater the number of them reported.

What are the limits of man's ability to retain information presented a single time? In a traditional memory-span experiment, a series of auditory or visual stimuli is presented at the rate of one item per second. As soon as the last item has been presented, the subject is asked to repeat the series in the order in which it was given. The number of items is varied to determine how many of them can be repeated without error half the time. This task closely resembles the everyday experience of looking up a telephone number.

The results of this experiment resemble those of the attention-span experiment. For college students, about seven or eight items is the average memory span (number of items correctly reported 50 per cent of the time). This finding supports the notion that the limits of attention and of memory are closely related. Memory span, like attention span, can with practice be enlarged to include up to ten or twelve items. Memory span also varies with the type of item the subject has to report. Experiments on both memory and attention span are rather complex and recent research has tried to devise simpler techniques for the analysis of memory capacity.

SENSORY STORAGE

The information provided by our senses is available not only for the duration of the event itself but also for a short while afterward. At the neurophysiological level, electrical phenomena associated with sensory stimulation of short duration, such as a click or a 1-millisecond flash, persist for at least several hundred milliseconds after the event. This is true in sensory projection areas of the brain as well as at the receptor level. At the behavioral level the persistence of positive and negative afterimages can be demonstrated. Other convincing evidence for the short-time continuation of sensory events comes from a phenomenon known as backward masking. An individual is presented with a stimulus that under normal conditions would be readily identified. Now, however, it is followed within a few milliseconds by another stimulus, more intense or more highly patterned. The effect of the first stimulus is masked so that the subject may not be able to identify it or, in some cases, even detect its presence.

Sperling (1963) used backward masking to study the rate at which new letters can be acquired from a visual stimulus. For different periods he exposed a slide which contained a number of letters and followed it with a masking stimulus consisting of random black and white squares. The masking stimulus serves to block any processing of information from afterimages which might occur if the field were dark. The results are shown in Figure 19. The number of letters reported correctly increases regularly with exposure duration, up to about 100 milliseconds. One additional letter is reported for every 10 or so milliseconds of exposure time. This is similar to the results for reporting the number of dots (page 62). Sperling also used a fixed 5-millisecond exposure of

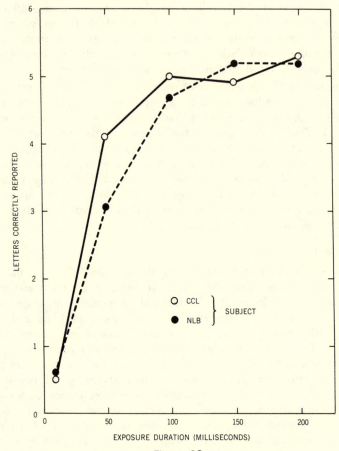

Figure 19

The number of letters correctly reported, as a function of the time between exposure of the letter slide and exposure of a masking stimulus. These functions are shown for two typical subjects. (After Sperling, 1963.)

the letters and varied the interval between that exposure and the presentation of the masking stimulus. Here again the number of letters reported increased at the rate of one for every 10 milliseconds' delay between the original and the masking stimulus. This finding is of critical importance. Since the stimulus slide is no longer present during the delay interval, it is obvious that the information it has given the subject has been preserved by him in a system that can be scanned at the rate of 10 milliseconds per item. This system, which preserves information prior to its being processed, is called the sensory storage system.

In an attempt to establish the characteristics of the sensory storage system, Sperling (1960) exposed slides consisting of up to twelve letters for 50 milliseconds. When the subjects were required to report all the information on the slide, they reported, on the average, 4.5 items. However, when they were instructed by an auditory signal after the slide was removed, to report only the letters in one row, their success was at the rate of 80-90 per cent. Since the row was chosen at random, it is possible to infer from this that at the time the slide was removed the subject had stored 80-90 per cent, or about 9 or 10 of the items. When a second was allowed to intervene before the instruction was given, the number of items in store dropped to about 4.5—the equivalent of the memory span. This experiment indicates that while the capacity of the sensory storage system is high the rate of loss of information from it is also high. The maximum capacity of the system is unknown, but must be at least 10 items, while the maximum duration seems to be of the order of 1-2 seconds, with the fastest rate of loss occurring in the first half second. The duration of this sensory storage system depends heavily upon the duration and intensity of exposure and the degree of masking imposed by subsequent fields.

The work of Broadbent (1958) on presentation of information to the ears argues for a similar system of auditory memory. In that experiment, the information presented to one ear was preserved during the processing of information to the other ear (page 58). The maximum delay between the two presentations in that experiment was 1.5 seconds. As was suggested earlier, sensory storage systems also have to be assumed in order to explain man's ability to report information arriving at unattended channels.

SHORT-TERM MEMORY

After a stimulus has been received and processed, there is a period of time during which it requires the attention of the subject if it is to be preserved. This time varies, depending upon the complexity of the stimulus. If a single item is presented, no further attention may be required for relatively permanent storage. If the number of items exceeds the memory span even very active rehearsal will not be sufficient to preserve them, since some of them will be lost during the rehearsal process. Short-term memory is defined as a system which loses information rapidly in the absence of sustained attention. Contrast the effect of distraction on the ability to recall your own phone number with its effect on you when you look up a new number, you forget the new number but retain your own. Short-term memory involves about the first sixty seconds after presentation of a new stimulus. After that time, either the items are lost or they are transferred to a long-term memory system.

The questions of major interest with respect to short-term memory are as follows: First, what is the overall capacity or amount which can be stored in the system? Second, at what rate is information lost from it if rehearsal is prevented? Third, what is the relation between this system and long-term storage? The answers to these questions require a review of evidence from a variety of experiments.

The number of items retained after a single presentation is derivable from the memory-span experiment (page 60). However, the memory span may be a low estimate of the short-term memory capacity, since information from later items tends to be lost during the act of recalling earlier items. In one technique in which the subject is required to monitor a series of digits and report only which digit is missing, the obtained span was about one and a half times the memory span from the same subjects (Buschke, 1963).

The type as well as the amount of material affects the capacity for short-term memory. For example, the memory span for letters is 7 items, while the memory span for simple words is 5 items. The number of letters retainable when they are grouped into words is increased several fold. Similarly, subjects can remember eleven binary digits and eight decimal digits, though eleven binary digits can be represented by only four decimal digits. George Miller (1956) pointed out that man shows relatively better retention of complex items such as words than simple items such as letters. Thus, the number of letters retained increases if the subject can find simple words which tie together a number of unrelated letters. Miller proposed that the limitation on human memory be thought of in terms of number of *chunks*, or meaningful units. The memory span is longer for simple chunks than for complex chunks. Simple chunks, however, convey less information than complex chunks. To convey maximum information it is better to use complex chunks. In the next chapter the method of measuring the information in a chunk will be discussed.

In the memory-span experiment, the subject is obliged to preserve the order of items as well as the items themselves. Temporal order is difficult to retain. One of the advantages of storing information in a few complex chunks rather than in many simple ones may rest upon the ease of keeping the order of a relatively few items. A recent investigation (Crossman, 1960b) supports this notion.

In summary, the capacity of short-term memory is limited to a relatively few chunks. The amount of information which can be conveyed to the subject within that limitation will depend upon the language which is used to formulate the chunks and the subject's skill in using that language.

A second question concerning short-term memory is the rate at which information is lost. When you look up a phone number and then begin to dial it, even a brief interruption may cause you to lose the number. This phenomenon has been explored in the laboratory. Peterson and Peterson (1959) presented subjects with three unrelated letters, followed by a three-digit number. The subjects were required to count backwards by threes from the number for a variable period and then attempt to recall the letters. The findings are shown in Figure 20.

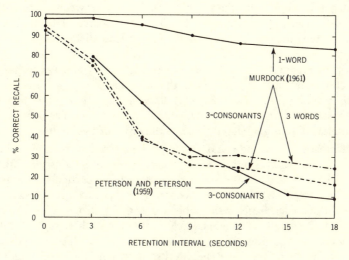

Figure 20

Retention of one word, three unrelated letters, and three unrelated words after a variable interval of backward counting. The names of the investigators originally reporting these data are shown in the graph. (After Melton, 1963.)

The proportion of perfectly recalled three-letter series falls to 20 per cent in 18 seconds. Thus, in the absence of rehearsal, only a small number of items can be retained in their correct order—and then only for a brief period. Figure 20 also includes data from Murdock (1961), who used three unrelated letters, one word, and three unrelated words as stimuli. In accord with Miller's chunking notion (page 66), three unrelated words and three unrelated letters gave similar results.

When the number of items to be recalled approaches the memory span the decline in percentage of correct recalls is even more marked. Conrad (1960) showed that even a momentary interruption in rehearsal is sufficient to cause retention of eight-digit series to drop by half. When the number of items to be recalled is beyond the memory span, the percentage of correct recalls declines over time even without any interruption of the subject's rehearsal. This has been shown by Anderson (1960) for periods up to 30 seconds.

Letters and other verbal materials are easily rehearsed by covert repetition. By way of contrast, Poulton (1963) studied retention of a complex, irregular wavy line, which the subject had to follow with a pencil. He found that accuracy in reproducing the reversals in the track depended upon the time allowed to elapse between presentation and recall, even when subjects were free to rehearse. This finding is important since aspects of many skills do not lend themselves to covert repetition.

Not all memory of a stimulus is lost rapidly, even when rehearsal is difficult. Some information about the stimulus is retained for a very long time and in the face of great interference from other activity. When a subject forgets a telephone number, he is not likely to forget it completely. Often he will only change the order of two digits.

Information may fade and become inexact rather than be wholly lost from short-term store. A *B* is more likely to be misremembered as a *P* than as a *J*. This aspect of retention is particularly striking when the subject is allowed to recognize rather than recall previous stimuli. In one such experiment (Shepard and Teghtsoonian, 1961) subjects were presented with cards, each containing a three-digit number. They were then required to state whether or not the number had appeared earlier in the list. The results, shown in Figure 21, indicate that the probability of being correct was significantly above chance, even when several minutes and sixty different numbers intervened between a given number and its repetition. This illustrates the persistence of some aspects of stimuli which have been presented only a single time.

The third major question about short-term memory has to do with the conditions under which information in it is transferred to the long-term store. Such transfer is necessary to account for the remarkable persistence of some information about a stimulus. Retention in long-term memory, however, is not necessarily permanent. Rather, such information is subject to loss through interference from prior and subsequently learned material which is similar to it. However, the rate at which information is lost from long-term store is much lower than that from short-term store and, once material has reached the long-term

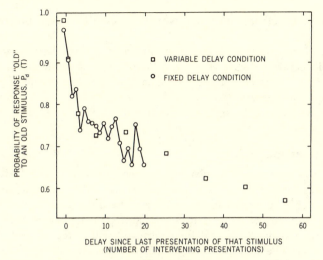

Figure 21

The probability of recognizing a three-digit number seen before, as a function of the number of new numbers intervening between the original presentation and the re-presentation of the number. The open circles are for conditions in which the number of intervening items was fixed for a block of trials and the squares represent a condition in which the intervening instances varied from trial to trial. (After Shepard and Teghtsoonian 1961.)

system, it is not subject to loss merely by the absence of rehearsal. It therefore does not depend upon the active attention of the subject.

It has already been pointed out that the smaller the amount of material presented to the subject the more likely it is to reach the long-term storage system. In addition, the longer the subject is free to rehearse the information, the more likely he is to store it permanently. In many laboratory experiments on verbal learning the subject is presented with the same information for many trials, and this process is meant to insure its reaching long-term store. Finally, novel or fresh information has a greater chance of reaching long-term store. For example, it has been shown that three items presented on the very first trial of an experiment show little or no loss even after a long period of non-rehearsal (Keppel and Underwood, 1962). The slow forgetting on the first trial of a memory study is in marked contrast with the rapid forgetting reflected in Figure 20, which represents a large number of trials.

The interpretations contained in this section have been based on a clear distinction between short- and long-term memory systems. Some psychologists do not accept this distinction and prefer to think of short- and long-term memory as parts of a single system. The empirical results, however, are the same, whichever of the two theoretical frameworks they may be considered a part of.

SERIAL MEMORY TASKS

Many memory tasks involve continuous presentation and retrieval. These tasks require a combination of short- and long-term memory processes. They are particularly important because most skills involve keeping a running account of events occurring in the perceptual field. This information is stored and then retrieved within the context of the serial activity. The study of tasks of this sort reveals aspects of memory which are not easily discovered in the simpler and more analytic techniques discussed so far.

Two general methods for studying these processes have been used. The first method, called the running memory span, involves the presentation of a string of unrelated items without any fixed end point. The subject either is required to recall the part of the series immediately before the experimenter stops or is provided with a cue as to which items out of the series to recall. The second method involves the use of skilled tasks such as typing or reading in which the subject's response naturally lags behind his acquisition of new information.

Results on the running memory span indicate that subjects can recall only the last three or four items of a list which is terminated suddenly (Pollack, Johnson, and Knaff, 1959). This figure represents about half of the normal memory span. Lloyd et al. (1960) presented subjects with a series of items divided into categories such as names of fish (trout, pike, etc.) or of trees (elm, oak, etc.). While the series was being presented to the subject, he would be cued with the name of a category and was required to recall the last item that had been presented in that category. In this situation, subjects were unable to attain 50 per cent correct responses if more than five items had intervened between the presentation of a given item and its being cued by its category name. These results indicate that the limitations of the running memory span are greater than those of the normal span.

A number of studies have been made of the lag between the intake of information by the eye or ear, and the response to that information. They usually deal with well-learned skills similar to those of everyday life. One of the first reports of this kind of running memory was included in the early study of telegraphic language by Bryan and Harter (1899). They reported that in receiving code, expert operators lag behind the message by three or four, and sometimes by as many as ten or twenty words. It is important to note here that we are dealing with the natural language, which is both highly familiar and highly predictable. Thus twenty words may actually constitute only a few separate "chunks."

Buswell (1927) studied the amount by which the eye leads the voice in reading (eye-voice span). For good readers, he found an increase from eleven letters in the second grade to about sixteen letters in the twelfth grade. Poor readers had a shorter span. According to Woodworth (1938),[*]

> The eye-voice span is very elastic. It goes down almost to zero when unfamiliar or ambiguous words are encountered; the eyes mark time until the meaning is discovered. Where the material reads along smoothly, the span lengthens and may become for an instant as long as a whole line of print. The span in terms of words varies from zero to eight. Measured in time, the eye-voice span for mature readers runs at about one or two seconds; the voice reaches a word one or two seconds after the eye has fixated it. (p. 733)

It is interesting to note that this one- to two-second lag in processing printed information compares to a minimum of about 0.4 seconds when an individual is asked to speak a random word as rapidly as he can after it is exposed.

Poulton (1958a) determined the maximum lag that was possible in dictation. Subjects printed the words they heard from tape recordings. The speed was increased so that the subjects fell farther and farther behind as they worked. Instructions were to go as far as possible, then skip and pick up the dictation at a later point. The experimenter measured how far behind subjects were able to lag before they had to skip. The results showed that on a first hearing, the best performance for a group of subjects averaged about thirty-five letters, while the best subject attained a span of fifty-four correct letters. These results indicate performance comparable to Bryan and Harter's telegraphers. In ordinary typing from copy, the eye-finger span (Butsch, 1932) is about three words and averages five or six letters. However, typing is a slower process than reading and the task is one that, except at very high levels of skill, emphasizes letter habits. The eye-finger lag in typing is about one second for moderately skillful typists.

[*]Robert S. Woodworth, *Experimental Psychology*, copyright 1938; Revised Edition by R. S. Woodworth and H. Schlosberg, copyright 1954. Holt, Rinehart and Winston, Inc., publishers.

The conclusion from all of these studies is clear. In organized activity, man can use his running-memory capacity to enhance performance, since it is possible to utilize the familiarity of the natural language for checking errors. There is, therefore, some gain to be achieved from storing a sequence of events before starting to respond to them. The lag in running memory is usually greater than a reaction time. It may be considerably greater than the memory-span data obtained from using random sequences. In cases where the natural language is used, it is clear that subjects are grouping or recoding stimuli into chunks on the basis of their familiarity with the material or the task. Running short-term memory is a component process in nearly every ordinary activity and thus is one of the most important factors in limiting skilled performance.

RESPONSE PROCESSES

The previous sections of this chapter have examined a number of limitations on man's ability to process and store information from the environment. In this section we shall examine the limits in the capacity for communication with the environment through responses. First we shall consider the number and accuracy of motor responses, then explore some of the limits to the rate and timing of motor responses in conjunction with similar limits on the stimulus side.

VARIETY

The variety of responses which man can make is indescribably large. Among the response systems most important for communicating with the environment are the hands and the vocal mechanism. Facial expressions also play an important role in communication, particularly of emotion. Movement of the arms and legs, as well as activities involved in the maintenance of posture, plays a key role in skilled activities. Moreover, these response systems are probably never employed in exactly the same way twice. It has been pointed out by a noted physiologist (Paillard, J., 1960, pp. 1683–84) that a detailed analysis of muscle movements indicates:

> The most significant fact revealed by this type of analysis of muscular activity is the extreme fluidity of the patterning of action, depending on the initial posture of the segments and on the nature of the resisting forces. The same final effect can be attained in a hundred different ways. A given movement can never be repeated identically. We can never find two patterns of activity repeated twice in succession which are strictly superposable. At the level of the muscle itself the spatiotemporal pattern of recruitment of the motor units implicated in voluntary movement is never absolutely identical.

While it would not be possible to describe the countless individual responses, it is possible to indicate limitations upon the success of motor response. The question can be phrased in terms of the accuracy of a response in producing outputs of various magnitudes and directions.

ACCURACY

The precision of a response with respect to magnitude and direction is limited by man's capacity to discriminate the muscular and visual feedback from the movement. Such discrimination is an absolute judgment which is subject to the same limitations as judgment from other sensory modalities. Whether a subject is asked to lift an object and estimate its weight or to push against a rigid stick with a specified number of pounds of pressure, the demands upon performance are similar. Data from such experiments indicate that capacity for absolute judgment of the magnitude and direction of movement lies well within the range discussed earlier for other sensory channels. Thus it appears that the limits of man's output are well matched to his sensory input capacities. It is important to note, however, that some gifted and highly trained individuals, such as baseball pitchers and musicians, may have developed unusual capacities for producing specific responses, in the same way that those with absolute pitch have developed unusual sensory capacities.

The notion that the precision of a response is limited by the accuracy of evaluating feedback information receives support from experiments employing augmented feedback to increase the discriminability of different movements. In such cases the ability to make fine adjustments increases. For example, Bahrick (1957) has shown that the addition of a spring to a control leads to improvement in the accuracy of blind positioning of the control, presumably because each increment in response amplitude now has associated with it a more easily discriminated change in force, resulting from displacement of the spring. In the same way, Helson (1964) showed that magnification of the error in a task which demanded fine adjustment led to improved performance in the task.

TIMING

The enormous number and complexity of particular responses make exact specification of single movements difficult. Here we only emphasize the commonalities in the central organization, the timing, and the rate of execution of responses, but the reader should keep in mind the differences and complexities of various response systems. There is always a delay between the occurrence of a stimulus and the initiation of a response to it. This delay is called the reaction time. Reaction time includes the interval during which neural impulses are conducted to and from the brain, but depends primarily upon processes in the brain itself. For this reason there is much similarity in reaction time for different sensory and motor systems.

Reaction time is approximately 20-30 milliseconds faster for hand movements than for foot movements; both these values fall within the range of 140 to 180 milliseconds. The differences can be accounted for largely by the distance of the various limbs from the brain. Reaction time for such diverse response movements as contracting the finger, biting, and moving the eye are nearly identical. Despite the fact that muscular control of the eye is much more complex than that of the foot, for example, reaction time for these responses varies only slightly when corrected for distance from the brain. In addition, the same people who tend to be quick in making hand movements are quick in making foot, eye, or biting movements (Woodworth and Schlosberg, 1954). This also indicates that reaction time primarily represents a central process characteristic of the individual.

Reaction time for different sensory stimuli also exhibits considerable commonality. The reaction times for sound, touch, and electric shock stimuli are almost identical. Over the range of intensities studied, however, the reaction time to light generally seems to be about 20 per cent higher. This may reflect delays in the photochemical processes which convert light into electrical energy.

Reaction time represents a delay due primarily to the organization of the response. These delays will be considered in greater detail in Chapter 6. Given that reaction time represents a minimum interval in the initiation of a response, how accurately can man time his responses above this interval?

Recent studies by Richard Pew (1965) seem to provide an answer to this question. Subjects were trained to press a key at a fixed interval after a warning signal. The interval is well above the reaction time of the subject, so that the only issue is the accuracy of timing. Feedback is provided on whether the subject is within a criterion interval surrounding the correct time. The criterion interval is reduced over days in order to force the subject to time more and more accurately. With a target time ranging from 250 to 700 milliseconds, the results of the studies indicate that two-thirds of a subject's responses are within ten per cent of the target time, and 95 per cent of his responses are within 20 per cent. Thus, with a target time of 350 milliseconds, two-thirds of all responses will fall within the range of 315-385 milliseconds and 95 per cent of all responses will fall within the range of 280-420 milliseconds. If the target time is doubled the range of responses is also doubled. The degree of accuracy appears to be a constant percentage of the target time, at least within the range of this study.

REPETITION

Each sense modality seems to have specific mechanisms designed to use information derived from small temporal differences. In audition, for example, if a click is presented to each ear and if the clicks are within approximately a millisecond of each other, the subject will report a single click coming from a position in space which depends on the temporal interval between the clicks. This information is important in localizing objects in space in order to orient in the direction of a sound. This particular mechanism is specific to audition and works only when the stimuli are very close in time. The mechanism allows the organism to use information involving temporal differences of less than a thousandth of a second. A related mechanism in the visual system produces the impression of motion when discrete stimuli at different locations occur within approximately 60-100 milliseconds (Wertheimer, 1925). Thus, the perceptual quality of experience arising from stimuli presented in close temporal proximity may vary considerably from one sensory modality to another.

By causing a stimulus to recur at close intervals, we can study man's capacity to tell whether or not the stimulus is interrupted or continuous (temporal resolution). This capacity is the basis for the perception of flicker in vision, flutter in audition, and vibration in the tactile sense. The frequency at which a light will begin to flicker, for example, varies from about ten cycles per second for low intensities to about one hundred cycles per second for very high intensities.

Hirsh and Sherrick (1961) conducted a series of tests using visual, auditory, and tactile stimuli in various pairings, in order to determine how large the interval between stimuli had to be before the subject could tell reliably which stimulus had come first. For this, the interval had to be considerably greater than for the simple detection of an interruption. The particular pair of sense channels to which the stimuli were presented appeared to make no difference in the results.

The probability of correctly giving the order in which pairs of stimuli are presented is shown in Figure 22 as a function of the time interval between the two stimuli. Data are shown for auditory, visual, and tactile stimulus pairs. The designation of the stimulus as "left" and "right" is arbitrary. The authors concluded that in order for judgments to be correct 75 per cent of the time an interval of 20 milliseconds between the presentation of two stimuli was necessary. Warrick (1961), however, found a longer interval necessary. Subjects in his study required a 50-millisecond interval in order to score correctly 75 per cent

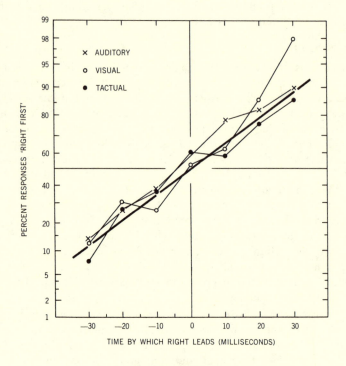

Figure 22

The percentage of the time that subjects identify the "right" stimulus as the one which arrived first as a function of the interval by which the "right" stimulus leads the "left." The designations "left" and "right" are arbitrary. Stimuli in three different sensory modalities are used and the common function illustrates the generality of the mechanisms which serve to discriminate temporal order. (After Hirsh and Sherrick, 1961.)

of the time and, for 95 per cent a 100-millisecond interval. The theoretical implications of these findings are obvious. The data indicate that judgments of prior arrival are made by some central mechanism into which come signals from different senses. This contrasts with the modality specific mechanisms discussed above (p. 75). Furthermore, differential time constants for different senses, assuming they exist, do not appear to affect the central decision maker, since there was no tendency for stimuli delivered to one sense channel to be consistently judged prior to events in another channel. The exact intervals required for 95 per cent correct judgments seem to vary between the two studies, but are less than 100 milliseconds.

A more complex task which also provides an analysis of man's temporal resolving power involves keeping track of the number of events in a sequence. Cheatham and White (1954) presented a series of rapid clicks at rates varying from ten to thirty clicks per second. Their

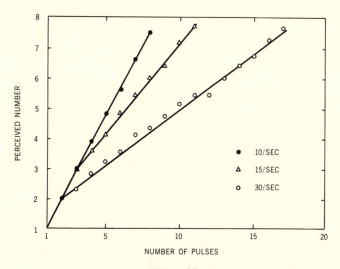

Figure 23

The number of pulses reported by subjects, as a function of the number of pulses actually presented at three different rates of presentation. These data illustrate that the number of pulses heard depends not on the number presented but on the total time it takes to present them (see text). (After Cheatham and White, 1954.)

major finding is shown in Figure 23, which plots the perceived number of clicks against the actual number presented in the series. Notice that subjects always report fewer clicks than actually occur. The subjects were not, however, simply guessing. Their perception of the number of clicks was remarkably consistent. In general, for each .1-second increment in total time subjects reported one additional click, regardless of the actual rate at which the clicks were occurring. Thus for a half-second period, whether five clicks were presented in the 10-per-second rate or fifteen clicks at the 30-per-second rate, the perceived number was about five. There is a slight tendency for the perceived number to increase with the rate, but that increase is much smaller than the increase with time.

White (1963) showed that similar functions are obtained for other sensory modalities. Figure 24 shows the relation of actual stimuli to

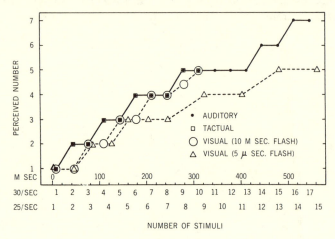

Figure 24

This curve illustrates the same function as the one in Figure 23 but it represents several different sensory modalities. Again the total number of .100-second intervals rather than the number of stimuli presented determines the number reported. (After White, 1963.)

perceived stimuli for visual, auditory, and tactile modalities. The similarities between modalities with respect to the actual-perceived relationship are far more striking than the differences.

These data agree that the rate at which relatively simple stimuli are received is about 10 per second. When rates are greater than 10 per second, subjects tend to report as a single stimulus all stimuli which occur within a .1-second interval.

Temporal limitations are also apparent in the rate at which responses are generated. The maximum rate of response is also about ten per second. The limit for repetitive movement of the hand, foot, or tongue, for example, is about ten movements per second. The maximum rate is slower for limbs with large mass, but only slightly so and not nearly in inverse proportion to the mass. The maximum rate at which the vocal mechanism produces short words, phonemes, or letters is less than ten per second, and the rate of vibrato in singing is ten vibrations per second. The eyes, which normally come to rest between move- ments, can make a maximum of about five movements per second, and the eye and the hand working together can track a moving object through four or, at most, five movements per second. Keeping track of the number of prior stimuli and responses is often essential to the generation of movements. The limits on discrimination of prior arrival agree fairly well with man's capacity for generating rapid sequences of responses, and probably for much the same reason; that is, some inherent limitation on central regulation of temporal relations. For example, Fenn (1938), commenting on the ten-per-second limit on the frequency of motor responses, pointed out that the muscles, viewed only as sources of energy, were capable of moving the limbs at much faster rates. He concluded that the frequency limit was established by the capacity of a central control system to regulate the timing of nerve impulses sent out over the motor pathways which maintain the sequence of muscular contractions and relaxations.

These temporal limitations lead to the possibility that a continuous stream of incoming information is quantized, or dealt with in discrete time intervals, by the nervous system. The frequency with which the ten-per-second or 100-millisecond figure recurs is highly suggestive of the operation of such a mechanism. There is sufficient variability in the data to leave it uncertain as to whether this is a fixed phenomenon, or simply an average of a range of intervals. From the standpoint of sensory psychophysiology, Robert Boynton lends additional support to the quantizing suggestion. In a paper which reviews temporal factors in vision (1961), he comes to the conclusion that

a common unifying principle, apparently consistent with the data, is the idea of temporal quantization of the visual input by the higher visual nervous system, so that the input is "packaged" into discrete time frames within which a purely temporal discrimination is not possible (page 753).*

His argument for assuming that quantization is imposed at some level of the nervous system beyond the receptor is based on data showing that retinal processes respond to temporal variations of the stimulus at rates at least up to 30 per second, even though phenomena such as apparent motion (page 75) occur at half this rate.

*Reprinted from "Some temporal factors in vision," by Robert M. Boynton, in *Sensory Communication,* edited by Walter A. Rosenblith, by permission of the M.I.T. Press. Copyright 1961 by the Massachusetts Institute of Technology.

REFRACTORY PERIOD

An even more severe temporal limitation to man's performance appears when responses are required for each of two successive signals. In this situation, the second of the two signals shows a longer than normal reaction time. The extent of the delay in the response to the second signal decreases with the interval between the signals. This phenomenon (Welford, 1952) has been called the *psychological refractory period.*

The refractory-period notion suggests that there exists some mechanism which is limited in its capacity to process signals. This viewpoint is in accord with the notion of a limited capacity for attending to simultaneous events. As was pointed out earlier, two simultaneous signals may be handled together provided that there is little uncertainty about the time of their arrival or about the responses to be made to each of them. However, once the mechanism is fully committed to the processing of one signal and to the preparation of the response to it, no other signal can be handled until the mechanism is cleared.

The quantitative limits of the refractory period are not completely known. In most experiments the extra delay in the reaction time to the second signal is not quite equal to the time between its presentation and the initiation of the response to the first signal. This indicates that at least the peripheral conduction of the second signal can proceed while the first signal is being processed. It has been suggested (Welford, 1952) that the second signal is also delayed during the processing of proprioceptive feedback from the first signal. There is little conclusive evidence on this point. However, the fast rates of continuous movements make it appear likely that processing of new information can partly overlap responses to prior signals.

Besides the idea of a limited capacity mechanism, two alternative explanations for the delay in reaction time have been offered. The first suggests that delays of the second signal are caused by peripheral interference on either the sensory or the motor end. The second suggests that delays of the second signal are due to the subject's failure to expect a second signal so shortly after the first.

Studies by Davis (1957) and Creamer (1963) present evidence against either of these explanations. They have shown that the refractory period occurs even when one signal is visual and the other auditory and when the responses are with the opposite hands. These arrangements minimize peripheral interference. In addition, Creamer (1963) has shown that the refractory phenomenon also occurs when the subject undergoes a block of trials with a fixed interval between signals, so that he comes to expect them to occur in rapid order.

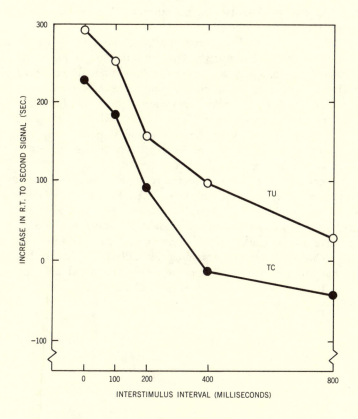

Figure 25

The increase in reaction time to the second of two signals, as a function of the interval between the signals. The open circles represent a condition in which the intervals varied from trial to trial (Temporal Uncertainity) and the closed circles represent intervals which were fixed for a block of trials (Temporal Certainty). These curves illustrate the psychological refractory period (see text). (After Creamer, 1963.)

Both Davis (1957) and Creamer (1963) found that the second signal showed significant delays out to an interval of about 250 milliseconds between the two signals. Figure 25 shows the extent of the decrement in reaction time for the second of two signals as a function of the interval between the signals. The two lines represent temporally certain and temporally uncertain conditions.

The refractory period indicates limits to the rate at which man can respond to successive stimuli. The limitation on responses to successive stimuli are much greater than the limitations discussed for discrimination between stimuli or for keeping track of successive sensory events. Since most skills involve responses, this limitation plays an important role in determining the level of skill which man can reach. Moreover, if the processing of the first signal is particularly complex, the refractory interval appears to increase. The consequences of this limitation will be developed in Chapter 6.

This section concludes the summary of evidence concerning the component processes involved in skills. This chapter has attempted to provide a basic picture of man's limitations in sensory, perceptual, memory, and response functions. It should be borne in mind that all skills involve a combination of these component functions in very complex ways. Moreover, the performance of skills is not static, but constantly changing over time with increases in learning and shifts of motivation. In Chapters 6 and 7 an attempt will be made to analyze skills into these component processes.

5

In the last chapter, an effort was made to analyze basic human capacities. The next two chapters will deal specifically with perceptual-motor and language skills, analyzing their component processes. In this chapter, however, it will be necessary to discuss the method to be used in measuring performance.

TYPES OF TASKS

A distinction may be made between three different temporal patterns of stimulus events. Events are said to be *discrete* if they have a clearly defined beginning and end. Much of the knowledge available in experimental psychology concerns discrete stimulus events, such as the presentation of a single light or tone and discrete responses, such as the press of a lever or a single word.

Even discrete events have dynamic aspects. Stimuli always occur in some kind of context both spatial and temporal. Responses to a new stimuli are always superimposed upon ongoing behavior—the basic bodily processes, postural adjustments, etc. Thus, even in discrete tasks, "stimulus" and "response" are convenient abstractions from and simplifications of the real world of dynamic events and ongoing behavior. Judged by the neural and muscular activity involved, even so simple a response as a lever push is a complex pattern never exactly reproduced.

Stimulus or response events are said to be *serial* when the beginning and ending of units can be identified but events follow each other in rapid sequence. Reading is a serial task when viewed in terms of eye movements. In reading, the eye remains fixed for periods of 200 milliseconds or longer, and these periods are separated by short, saccadic movements lasting less than 40 milliseconds. If the subject receives information about future events, a serial task allows for the preparation of the next movement to be made while the last movement is being executed.

Finally, stimulus events may be *continuous*. A moving object, for instance, presents continuous information. In most studies of tracking behavior the subject is presented with a stimulus course which varies continuously. In these tasks the subject is required to make corrections so as to keep the system in a balanced state. Driving an automobile is a familiar tracking task. Whether the corrective responses made by man in such a task are ever actually continuous is a question to be considered in Chapter 6. In the last chapter it was shown that man is limited in his ability to respond to rapidly occurring signals. Tasks which present continuous information place severe demands upon this ability.

OPTIMAL MEASURES

An experimental analysis of skills depends upon the method chosen to measure performance. Consider the skill of the baseball batter. No single measure captures all aspects of his performance in that skill. The batting average is the most frequently used measure, but a clean-up hitter might be selected because of his ability to hit a long ball. This ability might be reflected in a relatively low batting average but a large number of total bases per hit. Or a good batter might be one who hits frequently with men on base, giving a high number of runs batted in. A leadoff hitter might be selected who walks frequently, perhaps scoring a large number of runs but having a low batting average.

The psychologist is often characterized as having a "black-box" or stimulus-response approach to behavior, in that his observations are restricted to sequences of events in the individual's environment and to observable response sequences. However, as is evident from the case of the batter, there are many ways to characterize such input-output relations, and some of these are much more valuable than others in revealing important aspects of human skills.

Among the more valuable characteristics of a system of measurement adequate to the investigation of skills is sensitivity to input, output, and the relation or balance between input and output. The only reason that the batting average is a useful measure is that over the course of a season each batter faces a large number of the available pitchers. A batter may have a wonderful average, but if he has yet to face strong pitching it is meaningless. In order to understand the meaning of the output (batting average) we must understand the meaning or quality of the input (quality of pitching faced). In order to describe the course of improvement in skills and to compare skills, it is necessary to capture the degree to which the output reflects the stimulus input.

A second criterion for a system of measurement is that it should be appropriate to the three types of tasks outlined above—discrete, serial, and continuous. It should also allow meaningful comparisons between performances in these situations.

Next, the measure should be sensitive to the accuracy of the responses made by the subject. The batting average, for example, is sensitive only near the region of the criterion. That is, it is sensitive to hits as opposed to outs but is not sensitive to the difference between a strikeout and a well-hit line drive that is caught. To be appropriate for all levels of skill, a measure should be sensitive to different aspects of performance even when these are far from the criterion used to define success.

The measure should take into account the length of time taken to perform a skill as well as the accuracy with which it is performed. Most skills depend at least partly on timing. In addition, time is a continuous measure and can discriminate between performances, even when a skill is so poorly performed as to give 0 per cent correct responses or so well learned as to give 100 per cent. More important, a measure must be sensitive to time because man is often able to vary his accuracy in proportion to the amount of time he takes to perform a task. A typist can go fast and make many errors or go more slowly and reduce error. Neither time nor accuracy alone can be used to compare the performance of two typists, but the two together can be.

Finally, the measure must be very general if it is to be useful in both perceptual-motor and language skills. Such generality may be somewhat at a disadvantage in particular cases but it allows for the broadest investigation of human skills.

INFORMATION TRANSMISSION

No single measure can meet all the criteria perfectly. In earlier chapters, many different types of measurement were introduced for the purpose of analyzing specific problems. These measures are as different from each other as, on the one hand, the time it takes to roll a cigar and, on the other, the number of digit-series reproduced correctly 50 per cent of the time. Each of these measures is appropriate within the context in which it was used. This chapter develops the concept of the rate of information transmission as a means of measuring skills. Like all measures, it summarizes certain aspects of performance and ignores others. In recent years, however, it has proved to be useful for comparing a variety of skills and has provided us with a more general picture of man's abilities and limitations.

The idea of man as a transmitter of information has already been introduced a number of times in this book. Up to this point, however, the ideas used have been mostly in accord with common-sense notions of what information is and how man uses it in making responses. It is now necessary to present in a more detailed manner a system for the measurement of information. The development here is intuitive rather than rigorous. More complete treatments of the subject are available in Attneave (1959) and Garner (1962).

AMOUNT OF INFORMATION

"Information" implies a gain in knowledge in some manner. A technical definition of the term, as developed in communication engineering (Shannon and Weaver, 1949), is both more precise and less general. In order for information to be conveyed, there must be uncertainty. The amount of information potentially available increases with the amount of uncertainty in the situation. The statement that 2 plus 2 equals 4 conveys no information to most of us because there is no uncertainty about the relation to begin with. The assertion that the result of a coin flip was "either heads or tails" conveys no information, because it does not reduce our genuine uncertainty about the outcome. However, the simpler statement "it is tails" does convey information.

How much information is there in a statement? The amount of information increases with the number of possible things which might have occurred. Thus there is more information in a statement that a die came up four than that a coin came up tails, because six things could have occurred with the die and only two with the coin. There was, to begin with, more uncertainty with respect to the die. The amount of uncertainty then increases with N, where N is the number of possible things which might have occurred.

Consider the case of coin flipping. If one coin is flipped, either of two things can occur; with two coins any of four things; with three coins any of eight things. As the number of coins increases by one, the number of alternatives multiplies in powers of two. Since one coin flip is like another, it is convenient to define information in a way which allows each flip to contribute equal information. The function which increases by equal amounts while N multiplies is called the logarithm of N. It is useful, therefore, to define information as the logarithm of N. The base of the logarithm is purely arbitrary. However, if information is to increase by one unit each time N doubles, the base 2 is proper. Since many systems have only two states, like coin flips or truth values or lights, the base 2 is convenient. Information (H), as defined in equation 1, is measured in units called bits (abbreviated from binary digits).

$$H = \log_2 N \tag{1}$$

In our examples so far, all the alternatives (N) in a given situation were equally probable. What happens when they are not? The statements that it will be cold in Alaska in January and that it will be warm in Alabama in August convey little information because they are virtually certain to be true. However, the reverse suggestion would convey much more information, since it is so improbable. Information should reflect the probability (p) as well as the number of alternatives (N). When the alternatives are equally likely, $p = 1/N$ or $N = 1/p$ and equation 1 may be made to read as follows:

$$H = \log_2 1/p \tag{2}$$

Notice that this equation is identical to equation 1 when it is the case that all events are equally likely.

In skills it is often the average information in a series of events which is desired. Each event contributes information in accordance with its probability. The amount of information contributed by each occurrence of an event is given by equation 2. However, any event occurs only as often as its probability (p). Thus, its weighted contribution to the total uncertainty is $p \log_2 1/p$. To calculate the average uncertainty (H) in the sequence, all these values are added together for each event (i), which gives equation 3.

$$H = \sum_{i=1}^{N} p_i \log_2 1/p_i \tag{3}$$

For example, consider a situation in which there are four lights with probabilities .1, .2, .3, and .4. Since one, and only one, light occurs on any trial, the probabilities add to 1. The average uncertainty about which event will occur in a sequence of such light flashes is shown below.

$$H = .1 \log_2 1/.1 + .2 \log_2 1/.2 + .3 \log_2 1/.3 + .4 \log_2 1/.4 \tag{4}$$

Figure 26 may be used for calculating the amount of information from equation 4. The figure gives the value of $p_i \log_2 1/p_i$ for all values of p_i. In order to solve equation 4 you first look up the value .1 on the x-axis of the figure. Follow the line through .1 vertically until you come to the curve and then read off the corresponding value (.32) on the y-axis. The same is done for the other possible values of i (.2, .3, and .4). These value are then added to yield the average information in the sequence, which is about 1.84 bits. Of course, Figure 26 is approximate. More exact calculation may be made from a table of logarithms.

INFORMATION TRANSMITTED

The information transmitted is that amount of the stimulus information which is represented in the subject's response. Information transmission will be maximum when one, and only one, response always

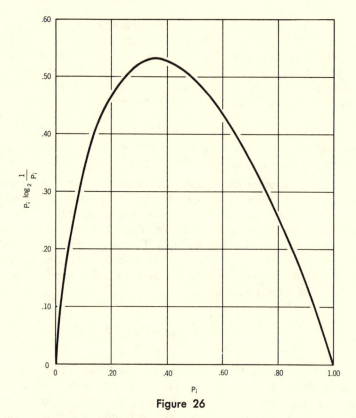

Figure 26

The curve shows $p_i \log_2 1/p_i$ for each value of
p_i. It may be used in the computation of infor-
mation (see text). (After Garner, 1962.)

occurs when a given stimulus is presented. If any other response occurs, the amount of information transmitted will be reduced.

To get a feeling for the calculation of information transmitted, look at Figure 27. In this Venn diagram the left circle represents the information in the stimulus, and the right represents the information in the response. In any example, the stimulus and response information can be calculated by use of equation 3 and Figure 26. If these two values are added, the sum includes all the information in the two circles: this includes the overlap of the two circles twice. The overlap information is represented twice in the sum since both circles include it.

One method of calculating information transmitted is illustrated in Table 2, using the example shown at the bottom of Figure 27. The figures in the cells represent the number of times each response occurs to each stimulus. Entries along the diagonal are correct responses. Table 2 shows first how to calculate the stimulus and response information for this example. Then the information in the cells $H(x,y)$, which is the total area of the two circles of the Venn diagram, is computed. Finally, this value is subtracted from the sum of the stimulus and response information to obtain the information transmitted, which is represented by the doubly shaded area of the Venn diagram.

For any situation in which a stimulus-response matrix of the type shown in Figure 27 can be developed, it is possible to calculate the information transmitted. Experiments on reaction time, absolute judgment, and memory are among those for which information transmitted can be calculated.

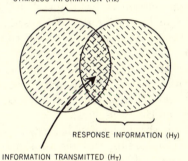

STIMULUS INFORMATION (Hx)

RESPONSE INFORMATION (Hy)

INFORMATION TRANSMITTED (HT)

	STIMULUS (x)				
RESPONSE (y)	A	B	C	D	SUM
a	0	5	0	0	5
b	5	10	5	0	20
c	5	5	15	20	45
d	0	0	10	20	30
SUM	10	20	30	40	100

Figure 27

The diagram portrays the relationship between stimulus, response, and transmitted information. The matrix below illustrates hypothetical data which might be obtained from an experiment.

Table 2

$H(x) =$ Stimulus Information
$= .1 \log_2 1/.1 + .2 \log_2 1/.2 + .3 \log_2 1/.3 + .4 \log_2 1/.4$
$= .33 + .46 + .52 + .53$
$= 1.84$ bits

$H(y) +$ Response Information
$= .05 \log_2 1/.05 + .2 \log_2 1/.2 + .45 \log_2 1/.45 + .3 \log_2 1/.3$
$= .22 + .46 + .52 + .52$
$= 1.72$ bits

$H(x,y) =$ Cell Information
$= 5(.05 \log_2 1/.05) + 2(.1 \log_2 1/.1) + .15 \log_2 1/.15 + 2(.2 \log_2 1/2)$
$= 5(.22) + 2(.33) + .41 + 2(.46)$
$= 3.09$ bits

$$H_T = \text{Information Transmitted} = Hx + Hy - H(x,y)$$
$$= 1.84 + 1.72 - 3.09$$
$$= .47 \text{ bits}$$

INFORMATION-TRANSMISSION RATE

The measures that have been derived so far have a number of important properties. They are sensitive to the number of alternative items which might occur on any trial. They reflect the degree to which the response is related to the stimulus. Finally, they are general, since they can be calculated whenever a set of events, each with a probability, can be specified. Moreover, they can be extended easily to take into consideration the speed as well as the information in the response.

When the information transmitted per response is divided by the time it takes to respond, the rate at which information is transmitted is obtained. The rate of information transmission is useful for all tasks which place emphasis upon speed. It can be used for discrete, serial, or continuous tasks. For the mathematics of information involving continuous input, see Shannon and Weaver (1949).

The amount of information transmitted and the rate of information transmission are measures which have most of the desirable properties listed earlier. They will be used in the remainder of this book for comparing various perceptual-motor and language skills.

Two disadvantages of these measures should be noted. First, these measures are not very useful when errors are of differential significance. The information measures do not differentiate between near misses and far misses. As long as one response always occurs to a given stimulus, information transmitted will be maximal and *any* departure will affect the measure equally. Second, information is defined only for a series of events where the probabilities governing the events are not changing. Since information is a function of the probability of events, it is usually necessary for the subject to have some knowledge of these probabilities. This knowledge may be obtained from instruction or from learning. Only when the subject's experience mirrors the objective probabilities can it be expected that information will be related to performance.

Information measures have many uses and are readily adapted to different aspects of performance. As the book progresses, some new applications will be considered and methods of calculating information provided.

REDUNDANCY

The measure of *redundancy* is one of the most useful provided by information theory. Redundancy (R) is calculated by means of equation 5.

$$R = 1 - \frac{H_{\text{actual}}}{H_{\text{max}}} \qquad (5)$$

H_{max} is the maximum value of information which that sequence of events can give. H_{actual} signifies the actual amount of information derived from a sequence of events. The maximum value always occurs when the elements in a sequence of N events are all equally likely to occur and when the occurrence of one event cannot be predicted from any previous event. When either of these requirements is violated, the actual information falls below the maximum, and the sequence is said to be redundant. The English language is redundant for two reasons. First, the probability of occurrence is not equal for all the letters: E, for example, is much more likely to occur than Q. Second, the probability of a letter's occurring is greatly affected by the letters which occurred previously. The redundancy of English has been computed (Shannon and Weaver, 1949) and the amount of redundancy of a language has been shown to be related to the rate of learning.

NOISE

In human behavior there is a great amount of apparently spontaneous variability. Engineers and information theorists call such variability, when it has to do with communication systems, *noise*. The amount of noise in a system can be specified in a statistical sense. In Figure 27, $H_{(y)} - H_{(T)}$ represents the amount of noise added to the response by the subject.

Just as it can be used to specify the amount of noise contributed by the subject, information theory can be used to show that there is additional information embedded in the noise. Errors made by man almost never are random; they are instructive for illustrating properties of his information-processing system. For example, when the letter P is forgotten in a memory experiment, there is a high likelihood that B, T, or another letter which sounds like P will have been substituted for it. The error contains information about the way in which man's memory system codes these items.

INFORMATION CODING

The concept of a code was introduced previously, in Chapter 2. Codes, as illustrated by various natural and artificial languages, are not peculiar to information theory. Nevertheless, information theory has brought added rigor to the study of codes. A code consists of a population or alphabet of symbols and a system of rules or constraints among them. The codes used in Chapter 2 were simple because they had no redundancy. The order of symbols to be presented to a subject was random. When rules are introduced which govern the order of symbols, such as in English, the code becomes redundant. Natural languages, which have many rules or constraints, are highly redundant. The linguist seeks to understand the rules, in the form of unit sequences and grammar, which produce the redundancy.

The idea of a code has wide application in the study of human information processing. Man has great ability in learning the rules of complex codes. More and more, biological and behavioral scientists are couching their theories in the terms of coding processes. We hear about the genetic code, a highly redundant code which determines inheritance. Theories of hearing are often expressed as a process by which physical signals are recoded by the ear into neural activity, the code of the nervous system. The study of codes and coding processes bridges the gap between many formerly unrelated areas, each attempting to describe an aspect of the living system.

CHANNEL CAPACITY AND HUMAN LIMITATIONS

The theory of information published by Shannon and Weaver (1949) set forth and elaborated upon the concept of the capacity of an information channel perturbed by noise. Three aspects of this development should be noted. First, the concept of channel capacity is a formal theoretical concept. Channel capacity is not something one measures directly but it is inferred as the maximum possible rate at which a channel can transmit information. Second, the idea of a channel includes a specification of the information code to be employed. If the code is changed, the capacity of the channel may change also. Third, the term channel capacity refers to the rate at which information is transmitted and not to the amount of information per response.

The concept of channel capacity as employed in information theory should not be confused with concepts regarding man's capacities and limitations. Man does have a limited capacity for many tasks. These limits were reviewed in Chapter 4. Some of man's capacities can be discussed in terms of the amount or rate of information transmission. However, there is not a single human channel capacity for all tasks and codes. It is not possible to predict on purely rational grounds the limits to the rate at which human beings process information. Instead, the limitations on many different aspects of processing have been analyzed from empirical studies (Chapter 4), and these will be used to describe and predict performance in complex tasks (Chapters 6 and 7).

HUMAN CAPACITIES IN PERCEPTUAL-MOTOR SKILLS 6

When you are waiting at a red light and the light changes to green, there is always a delay before you begin the sequence of responses that will move your car. The delay between the occurrence of a stimulus event and the initiation of a response to it is called the *reaction time*. All tasks which involve man's taking information from the environment and responding to it show some finite reaction time. Reaction time is that period during which the initial response is being prepared. Its components consist of the detection of a stimulus and the selection of an appropriate response. The selection may be more or less rapid, depending upon the degree of uncertainty about what the stimulus is and the compatibility between the stimulus and the response codes. In the early stage of a reaction-time task, the roles of attention, recognition, and memory may be critically involved. Because of these factors, the length of the reaction time serves as an index for gaging the component processes discussed in Chapter 4.

HISTORY OF REACTION-TIME STUDIES

Before we consider in greater detail the factors which affect reaction time, it will be worthwhile to examine, briefly, the interesting history of the study of the concept. It is only relatively recently that the phenomenon of reaction time has been recognized. The early Greeks had well-developed theories of the senses and of motor responses, and by the end of the classical period Galen had a reasonably precise notion of the reflex arc. Yet one looks in vain for a suggestion that man's response to a stimulus is necessarily delayed. In fact, until the nineteenth century the rate at which impulses are conducted along the nerves was frequently thought to be infinite.

SPEED OF THE NERVE IMPULSE

But as the nervous system began to be better understood, the idea that nerve impulses were conducted at an infinite speed was questioned. In the 1850's, Hermann von Helmholtz reported two ingenious experiments which demonstrated that the nerve impulse was relatively slow, although not nearly as slow as reaction time itself.

In one experiment, he stimulated a subject on the thigh and on

93

the sole of the foot and measured the delay in the responses. He then calculated the difference in reaction time between the two stimuli and on this basis concluded that neural impulses travel at the rate of 50 to 100 meters per second. Helmholtz also measured the time between the stimulation of the motor nerve of a frog and the twitching of its muscle, varying the distance between the point at which he stimulated the nerve and its attachment to the muscle. In this case, his estimate of the speed of neural impulses was approximately 25 to 50 meters per second.

Helmholtz's work on the speed of the nerve impulse is one of the earliest examples of establishing a relationship between physiological and behavioral facts. Subsequent research has confirmed his figure of 100 m/sec. for the great sensory and motor pathways in man. This figure makes it clear that most of the reaction time involves delays in the brain and not along the peripheral nerves.

THE PERSONAL EQUATION

But more than a half century before Helmholtz, astronomers had been aware of the importance of human reaction time. In astronomical observation it was necessary to record a star's transit to an accuracy of a tenth of a second. These observations involved the astronomer's using a metronome to determine the moment at which the star touched the cross hairs of his telescope. Since star transits are highly predictable events, it was possible to check one observer's data against those of another by taking observations on successive days.

It was as a result of such checks that, in 1794, Maskelyne, the chief astronomer at the Greenwich Observatory, noted a discrepancy of almost a second between his observations and those of his assistant. This discrepancy, which was highly consistent, led to the dismissal of the assistant and was reported in a scientific paper. Bessel, a noted astronomer who was also interested in errors of measurement, began to investigate the discrepancies between observers at various laboratories in Europe. He termed these discrepancies the "personal equation" and attributed them to processes within the observer. Bessel also discovered a number of the important properties of these individual discrepancies. For example, he showed that delays were shorter with the more intense stars, that they increased where events were unexpected, and that they were especially long when they involved simultaneous auditory and visual events.

These early data served as one basis for work in Wundt's laboratory on reaction time and on the processing of simultaneous visual and auditory events. Most of the findings of the astronomers were confirmed and form important aspects of present theories about reaction time.

SIMPLE REACTION TIME

Simple reaction time is the name assigned to the delay between the occurrence of a single fixed stimulus and the initiation of a response assigned to it. Since the work of the astronomers, it has been known that reaction time decreases as the intensity of the stimulus increases. Neither the speed of conduction along a neural fiber nor the amplitude of a given neural impulse varies with the intensity of a stimulus. The speed and amplitude of the nerve impulse itself are fixed characteristics of a particular nerve.

When a stimulus is well above the intensity at which it can be detected, and the subject has little uncertainty about when it will occur, why should the speed of his response vary with the intensity of the stimulus? In order to answer this important question, it is necessary to take a dynamic view of the process of stimulus detection. Remember that in the discussion of man's sensory capacity it was suggested that the presentation of a stimulus is always against some background or noise, either external or internal. It was also indicated that a stimulus does not yield precisely the same effect within the organism every time it is presented. Figure 13 shows that the effectiveness of a stimulus can be defined by a distribution of internal activity which overlaps with the distribution of effects due to noise or background alone. In experiments on sensory detection, the subject has unlimited time to make his decision concerning the presence or absence of a signal. Thus, his decision process can be viewed as a static one; he makes a *single* decision. If the activity which the stimulus causes is greater than some criterion set by the subject in accordance with the task assigned him, he reports a signal; if less, he reports none.

In a reaction-time experiment, however, speed is stressed; and moment-to-moment fluctuations in the information being conducted along the sensory nerves will affect the rate and accuracy of the decision-making process. In this case, therefore, the decision-making process must be viewed as dynamic—that is; as changing over time. The information being conducted over the sensory nerves is in the form of brief pulses of electrical activity separated by quiet intervals. When a signal is added to the noise or background activity, the rate of these pulses is increased. The response must be based upon the discrimination of this increase in rate of activity. However, the interval between neural impulses is not a constant property of the intensity of a stimulation but is also subject to noise. In order to decide whether or not a signal has occurred, it is necessary to sample a sufficient number of successive impulses to determine whether the present situation is more likely to belong to the distribution of noise intervals or the distribution of signal-plus-noise intervals. Naturally, the greater the intensity of the signal, the fewer the samples necessary for reaching a given level of confidence. This dynamic sampling of sensory information underlies the change in response speed with signal intensity. In this regard it is interesting to note that the rate of neural firing tends to be a logarithmic function of stimulus intensity and that the relation between reaction time and stimulus intensity also tends to be logarithmic over a considerable range. This tends to lend support to a model of the reaction-time task, in which man is viewed as making decisions based upon successive samples of the information coming from his sensory nerves. As this chapter proceeds, it will be necessary to show how such factors as attention, learning, and multiple signals affect the basic decision-making process. Before doing so, it will be instructive to examine the problems involved in measuring simple reaction time (RT).

These problems seem deceptively simple. All that appears necessary in order to measure simple RT is a stimulus, a timer, and a switch for the subject to use for responding. Unfortunately, the problem is a great deal more complicated than this list would suggest. Suppose the subject knows precisely when the stimulus will occur. For example, suppose it is always presented two seconds after a warning signal. The subject can time his response to occur almost coincidentally with the signal, thus reducing RT to close to zero. Of course, this is not what the investigator wishes. He desires the subject to be making his response preparation during the interval being measured. In order for this to happen, it is necessary to introduce some uncertainty about when or whether the signal will occur. However, the amount of uncertainty will change the performance of the subject. For example, if the subject is completely uncertain, as in the case of a very rare signal, he may produce very long RTs or miss the signal entirely (infinite RT). Therefore, there can be no fixed limit to the simple reaction time. The psychologist may, however, specify standard conditions of temporal uncertainty.

TEMPORAL UNCERTAINTY

Reaction time may approach zero if it is possible for an individual to anticipate an event. A baseball batter playing against a pitcher who always throws with the same speed can time his swing almost perfectly. Similarly, an automobile driver, as long as he can see the road ahead of his car, is able to time his steering motion to coincide precisely with variations in the road.

In Chapter 4 it was shown that man has considerable ability to time his responses to occur within a fixed interval. What happens when uncertainty is introduced about when, precisely, the signal will occur?

In this case, the response cannot be timed in advance but must be initiated by the signal.

Edmund Klemmer (1957) has investigated the role of temporal uncertainty in reaction time. He hypothesized that uncertainty could be varied in two ways. First, the length of the foreperiod (time between warning signal and signal to respond) could be increased. Since man's accuracy in estimating time varies inversely with the length of the interval, Klemmer reasoned that increases in the foreperiod would reduce the precision with which his subjects could predict the signal. Second, the foreperiod can be varied so that the subject cannot predict which of several different foreperiods will occur in a given trial.

Klemmer combined these independent manipulations into a single quantitative measure of uncertainty, using the system for measuring uncertainty (information) which was discussed in the last chapter. He added the uncertainty about the duration of the foreperiod and the uncertainty caused by the subject's limited ability to estimate the time-lapse accurately. This combined value (H_T), computed in bits, he

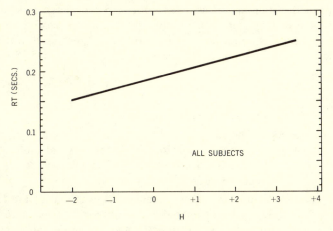

Figure 28

Reaction time (RT) as a function of the amount of temporal uncertainty (H). The temporal uncertainty combines the average length of the warning interval with its variability and is computed in bits. The reference position (0) is for a one-second fixed interval. Values of uncertainty greater than this are positive and those less than this are negative. (After Klemmer, 1957.)

plotted against the reaction time to the signal. A one-second interval served as a reference point; conditions with greater uncertainty than the reference are shown as positive and conditions with less uncertainty are shown as negative. Figure 28 shows the straight line which fits the data obtained in this study. The results provide a quantitative analysis of the effect of increasing the subject's uncertainty and thus requiring his attention to be sustained over varying time intervals. These results help to establish the view of attention as a graded phenomenon in delicate relation to the degree of uncertainty about the occurrence of a signal. The efficiency with which man can prepare to receive a signal varies with his certainty about the time of its arrival.

Before leaving the subject of temporal uncertainty, let us briefly examine an experiment where the interval between successive signals is very long. In this study (Warrick, Kibler, Topmiller and Bates, 1964), the interval was sometimes a matter of several days. After an initial period of adjustment, the subjects (secretaries who spent the time between trials engaged in the normal routines of their work) were able to press a key to turn off a buzzer in about .7 to .8 seconds following the onset of the stimulus. Thus, even with extremely large time uncertainty, simple reaction time apparently is well under a second in duration. Of course, this value is over three times as great as it would be if temporal uncertainty were reduced to the range which Klemmer considered.

CHOICE REACTION TIME

Simple reaction time involves only a single stimulus and response. It is a long way from such a skill to complex perceptual motor tasks. The next step is to consider reaction-time experiments with more than a single response (choice reaction time).

The earliest attempt to deal with choice RT was that of the Dutch physiologist Donders, who compared three different types of reaction time: *type-a* reaction, simple RT; *type-b* reaction, presentation of any one of five stimuli with a separate response to each stimulus; and *type-c* reaction, presentation of five stimuli, only one of which required a response. He found that RT was fastest for *type a* and slowest for *type b*. His theory was that each component function increased the reaction time by a fixed amount. The idea was that *type b* required both discrimination and choice, *type c* required discrimination but not choice, while *type a* required neither. Thus, by subtraction of c from b, he could obtain the choice time, and by subtraction of a from c he could obtain discrimination time. The basic findings of Donders are quite reliable and the theory is intuitively attractive, but it ran into difficulties for historical and scientific reasons. There are two major historical reasons. First, subsequent experimenters attempted to modify Donders' method so that subjects were required to signal when they thought a stimulus had been identified. This method (d-reaction) depended upon introspective analysis by the subjects, and the failure to obtain reliable results with this method tended to cast doubt on the whole enterprise. Secondly, interest in skills waned after the turn of the century. Psychologists turned their attention to animal and human conditioning and many of the promising results obtained earlier were ignored.

There were also three important scientific reasons that Donders' method was largely rejected. First, discrimination and choice time, like RT itself, are variable. Second, Donders' theory tended to suggest that discrimination and choice times did not vary with the situation and set given the subject. (Subsequent investigation in fact showed that such times depend upon a number of instructional factors.) Third, Donders' theory lacked a notion of change with practice. As we shall see, the appropriate model for reaction-time performance does depend upon level of training. For these reasons, the components of RT cannot be thought of as fixed constants. Nevertheless, the basic empirical work of Donders was correct, and his theory is clearly related to current conceptions of stages and levels in information processing.

Merkel (1885) extended Donders' data on the choice experiment to include a choice from among ten stimuli and responses. He found a logarithmic increase in the reaction time as the number of stimuli and responses increased. Not much was made of this finding, however, in 1885. But with the advent of information measures, Hick (1952) replicated the Merkel data and suggested that the rate of gain of information in this task is a constant. This conclusion involves a change of the axis in the Merkel experiment from number of alternatives to amount of information. Since information is a logarithmic function of number of alternatives, a straight line relates information and RT. The reciprocal of the slope of this function represents the rate of information transmission in bits/seconds. By itself this is not a new finding but merely a conversion of the scale and, therefore, implicit in the Merkel data. However, it was now possible to vary information in a number of ways to see whether the rate of information transfer remained constant with different methods of manipulating uncertainty.

In addition to varying the number of alternatives, there are several other ways by which one may vary information. Ways of manipulating temporal uncertainty were reviewed in the last section. Another method is to vary the probabilities among a fixed number of alternatives. In this method the subject is either informed or learns through experience that, for example, the probability of light A is .7 and of light B, .3.

In still another method the experimenter builds rules analogous to those of a simple grammar. For example, if light A occurs, the likelihood of light B following is .8, while that of light A following itself is .2. This method introduces redundancy (reduction of uncertainty) by providing sequential dependencies among the events. That is, the probability of an event depends upon the event that precedes it.

Hyman (1953) made intensive studies of the performance of four subjects in tasks which varied information through changing the number of alternatives, the probabilities, and the sequential dependencies. For each experimental condition he summarized the average information in bits and plotted it against the mean reaction time for that condition. The overall results for one subject are shown in Figure 29. As can be seen, the relation between information and RT is linear. The data from all three methods of manipulating information are closely fit by the same function. This finding indicates that the rate of processing a signal is a linear function of the amount of information in the stimulus sequence. It is an important extension of the Merkel data since RT is related not only to the number of alternatives but also to other important aspects of the stimulus situation. In the light of the discussion of individual differences at the end of Chapter 3, it is interesting to note that while the speed of response differs widely among Hyman's subjects, the linear relation between RT and information is common to them all.

Another experiment studied adjustments in the rate of processing signals that have differing probabilities (Fitts, Peterson, and Wolpe, 1963). The experimenters measured the reaction time to each of nine stimuli. On the first day the nine stimuli were equally likely. Starting with the second session, subjects were informed that one of the signals would be more frequent than the other eight. The results of the study are shown in Figure 30. Consider the top and bottom curves. The bottom curve represents a frequent stimulus, one with a probability .94, and the top curve represents the average of the other eight stimuli—each with probability of less than .01. The reaction time to the frequent stimulus in this condition reached 280 milliseconds by the fourth session, while reaction time to the eight infrequent stimuli averaged 450 milliseconds. In general, the subjects adjusted their speed to the degree of probability of the stimulus. Most of the adjustment occurred during the second session, but the process continued at a reduced rate over the four sessions. This finding illustrates that the ability to process a signal improves slowly as the subject becomes familiar with the probabilty with which that signal occurs within a given situation.

The second important finding of this experiment had to do with the speed of response to individual stimuli. So far, all data have con-

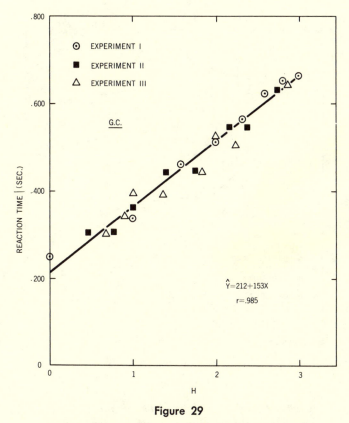

Figure 29

Reaction time for one subject as a function of information for three different methods of manipulating information. Experiment I involves changing the number of alternatives; Experiment II, changing the probabilities; and Experiment III, introducing sequential dependencies. (After Hyman, 1953.)

cerned the average reaction time as a function of the average uncertainty within the sequence. The average uncertainty reflects the probability that each individual stimulus will occur. For example, if there are two stimuli with probabilities of .7 and .3, respectively, the average information is .88 bits. This is the average of the two components, each with an uncertainty equal to $\log_2 1/p$. In this example the two component uncertainties are .51 and 1.71 bits. This means that the RT to the .7 stimulus should be faster than the RT to the .3 stimulus by just the amount predicted by the equation $RT = aH + b$.

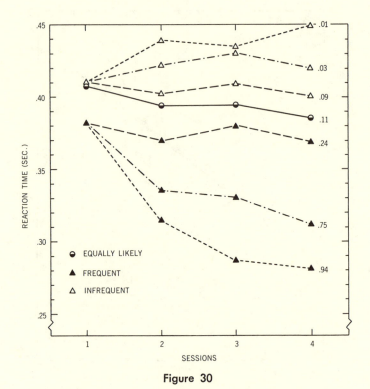

Figure 30

Reaction time over four days of practice to each of eight infrequent signals (top three curves) and to one frequent signal (bottom three curves). The middle curve (.11) represents a control condition in which all nine signals were of equal frequency. (After Fitts, Peterson, and Wolpe, 1963.)

In Hyman's experiment this expectation was not completely met. Reaction to the stimulus with the greatest uncertainty was slowest but not by as much as predicted from the equation. Figure 31 illustrates this same finding for the Fitts, Peterson, and Wolpe study. The graph shows the reaction time to *individual* component events as a function of their uncertainty. Notice that the linear relation holds up well in the middle of the range. However, the extreme points lie somewhat off the straight-line fit. In these data both the most frequent and the least frequent events are responded to somewhat too fast for the pre-

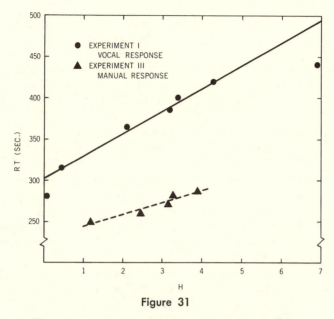

Figure 31

Reaction time as a function of information for component stimuli of differing frequency. The more infrequent the signal, the greater the information conveyed when it occurs and the longer the time taken to respond to it. The two curves represent two conditions of differing compatibility. The linear functions hold up well in the middle range but there are departures at the extremes. (Computed from data of Fitts, Peterson, and Wolpe, 1963.)

diction; that is, their RT lies below the straight line. These data indicate that the linear relation between uncertainty and reaction time holds up quite well at the middle ranges of uncertainty, but that there are departures at the extremes. No general formulation has yet been presented to handle these departures. In the next section, some other factors which affect this relation will be considered.

The data reviewed so far add to the picture of man as an information processor. In a simple RT task the major problem is to determine whether or not the rate of internal activity has changed so as to indicate a signal. The choice task adds to this a decision concerning which of several signals has occurred. The addition of event uncertainty requires the subject to search among the alternatives to produce the correct response. In Chapter 4 it was shown that the rate of such search is limited. In the initial stages of a search task the rate of response is a linear function of the number of items through which the search takes place. It is as if the subject compared the target to each successive item until he discovered a match. The choice reaction-time data, however, show a linear increase with the *logarithm* of the number of items. This represents a more efficient strategy in which each successive decision cuts the remaining alternatives in half. Each decision represents a one-bit reduction in uncertainty. Uneven probabilities bias this search process in favor of the alternative with the higher probability, and this alternative has faster RT.

Why should the search task and the choice reaction task show different effects of the number of alternatives, since both require a search among alternatives? The answer may lie in the amount of practice the subject has. Most of the search tasks reviewed previously (p. 59) have different items stored on each trial. The subject must continually search new sets. In this case the subject appears to search one item at a time. When a search task requires that the subject scan the same stored array on every trial and when practice is extensive (Neisser *et al.*, 1963) the function relating number of items to RT is flat. Since improvement is more rapid for the larger number of alternatives, at an intermediate stage of practice a logarithmic relation is to be expected. In fact, most choice RT tasks involve levels of practice far beyond those search tasks which have a new array on every trial. For this reason it is not too surprising that a more efficient search strategy than the linear one is apparent from the subject's performance. In the next section it is shown that some choice RT tasks can approach the flat function between number of alternatives and RT which Neisser *et al* found in their search task.

LEARNING AND COMPATIBILITY

The material reviewed so far has indicated uniformly a linear relation between reaction time and information for choice RT tasks. As the subject is required to respond to higher degrees of uncertainty his rate of responding slows down proportionately to the increase in information. The amount of increase in RT, however, depends heavily upon the task. Figure 32 illustrates results from a number of studies. In every case the relation between RT and information can be well described by a straight line, but the slope of that line may vary from 0 to 175 milliseconds per bit. The slope apparently depends upon two factors which have been discussed in some detail previously.

The first is the degree of compatibility between the stimulus and the response code. To illustrate this, let us consider some of the tasks

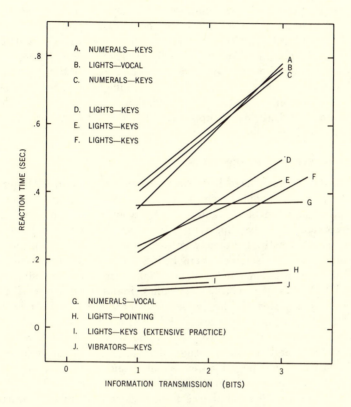

Figure 32

Reaction time as a function of information for a number of experiments of varying compatibility (see text). (Adapted from Fitts, 1964.)

which show very shallow slopes. Leonard (1959) (Figure 32, curve J) studied an RT task in which the subject rested his fingers upon vibrators and touched the vibrator which was activated. Mowbray (1960) (Figure 32, curve G) studied a voice reaction to arabic numerals. These two tasks show very little, if any, effect of increasing the stimulus information. On the other hand, Hick (1952) (Figure 32 curve F) studied a task in which the subject had to press one of ten keys when a light occurred, and Brainard *et al.* (1962) (Figure 32, curve B) used a numerical response to represent the spatial position of a light. These tasks give much larger slopes. Anything which tends to decrease the spatial or energy correspondence between the input and output so as to reduce compatibility will increase the slope.

For a given task configuration the slope will also vary with increased practice. Mowbray and Rhoades (1959) (Figure 32, Curve I), let one subject practice a key-press task for six months and found that the slope decreased steadily over time. The general finding is that the greatest improvement with practice will occur in those conditions which have the most uncertainty, thus tending to reduce the slope. Since compatibility rests on population stereotypes, which in turn depend at least partly upon learning, compatibility and learning effects are highly related.

HIGH LEVELS OF INFORMATION

The tasks which have been discussed and illustrated in Figure 32 all involve up to about 10 alternatives, or 3.3 bits of information. In this range there can be no doubt about the linear relation between RT and information. Above this range, however, no such simple relation can be asserted with confidence. Pollack (1963), using a task involving the naming of words which were briefly exposed by a tachistoscope, found a linear relation out to about 1,000 alternatives (10 bits), while Conrad (1962), using nonsense syllables, found a similar relation out to the 32 alternatives (5 bits) which was the highest number he used. Seibel (1963), using a key-press task which required all possible combinations of the ten fingers (10 bits), found very little or no increase in RT between 5 and 10 bits. He suggested that the function relating RT and information was negatively accelerated and approximated linearity only in the lower range. In addition, both Hyman (1953) and Fitts et al. (1963) have shown that extremely low probability alternatives which contribute large amounts of information (6-10 bits) are responded to more rapidly than would be predicted from the overall relation.

One reason for the confusion with respect to tasks which have high numbers of alternatives is the relative difficulty of producing a satisfactory stimulus-and-response code for such tasks. Stimuli like arabic numerals and responses such as the ten fingers make natural and familiar codes. However, when the experimenter chooses to produce a new and arbitrary code, the subject's behavior can present him with considerable problems. For example, in a recent study (Fitts and Switzer, 1962), three populations of stimulus items were used. The first were the digits 1 through 8; the second, the digits 1 and 2; and the third, the digits 2 and 7. The first population represented 3 bits of stimulus information (eight equally likely responses), while the others represented only 1 bit (two equally likely responses). During the first day of practice subjects using the first and third populations had an equal reaction time, while subjects using the second population gave faster responses. Thus conditions with 3 bits and with 1 bit gave equal speeds. However, after three days of practice the two groups using the 1-bit populations were equal and uniformly faster than the group using the 3-bit population. Apparently, it took a good deal of practice before subjects could learn to use the unfamiliar subset 2 and 7. At first they behaved as if all the numbers 1 through 8 could occur and it took three days before their behavior reflected the population of items which they were actually using. The problems of obtaining familiar S-R codes increase as the size of the desired population increases.

There appears to be a maximum or upper limit to times obtained in choice RT experiments of the type discussed in this chapter. Usually the RT lies below .6 to .7 second and rarely exceeds 1 second, regardless of the amount of temporal or event uncertainty in the stimulus. Tasks which have steep slopes (low compatibility) and high information show a departure from linearity at the upper end of the curve where the predicted RTs tend to exceed this maximum limit. In tasks with a relatively shallow slope, the relationship continues to be linear out to the highest amounts of information used, since the predicted value does not exceed the maximum limit. This analysis seems to describe much of the data using high information tasks. However, it does not tell us what mechanisms account for the maximum limit. Until experiments can overcome difficulties in stimulus-response codes for high information values, it is unlikely that an answer to this problem will be obtained.

RATE OF INFORMATION HANDLING

Man shows no fixed limit to the rate at which he can transmit information. He shows different rates of processing with different stimulus-response codes and different amounts of learning. Under some circumstances there is no increase in RT with increased information. Thus it makes no sense to talk about a fixed human capacity for processing information in choice RT tasks as it did in situations involving absolute judgment. However, the results of these studies indicate some important general characteristics of man as an information processor.

Two extreme models of skill in information processing can be suggested. The first views man as a collection of *independent* stimulus-response *associations* or reflexes. Each stimulus is hooked to an individual response through learning and does not interact with other stimulus-response pairs. In such a model, reaction time for a given association should not be affected by the occurrence of other associations. On the other hand, man could be thought to have a *single* processing *channel*, limited for a fixed amount of information per unit time. While neither of these views is likely to be held in such extreme form, the former is more closely associated with conditioning and strict S-R theory while the latter has arisen from perceptual experiments emphasizing the narrowness of human attention. In fact, the view of man emerging from the experimental laboratory is between these two models.

Early in training, particularly in tasks which have widely separate stimulus-response codes, man behaves almost precisely like a single channel limited for information. Numerous experiments confirm that in such circumstances the rate of information transmitted is a constant. Speed decreases in proportion with increases in information per stimulus. However, as man approaches more advanced stages of skill, and particularly when he reaches the highly automated final stage, he behaves much more like the pure reflex model. Speed becomes independent of the number of possible stimuli, and the rate of information processing approaches infinity as the slope relating speed to information reaches zero. This is not to suggest that the reflex model is correct in any anatomical or physiological sense, but only that in highly developed and highly compatible skills man behaves as if each stimulus-response connection were independent.

While the nature of human performance precludes fixing any theoretical limit to the rate of information processing in reaction-time tasks, it is often possible to develop practical limits. The practical limits apply where a particular code is used. Quastler and Wulff (1955) have studied the practical limitations on rate of transfer in several skilled tasks. The reason that such practical limits can be obtained is that most human tasks do not have infinitely large alphabets, but alphabets of fixed size. For example, there are only 26 letter keys on a typewriter, only 10 distinct Arabic digits, only 88 keys on a piano, and only a finite number of words in the typical English vocabulary. Thus even if man could in theory always achieve a higher rate of transfer by using a larger vocabulary, the fact that he cannot perform more than 10 responses per second, together with the finite limits of practical alphabets, imposes a limitation on him in his performance of most skilled tasks.

One experiment conducted by Quastler and Wulff used skilled pianists. The number of piano keys employed was varied from 3 to 65 keys. The rate of information transmission was studied as the population of keys and rate of response pacing were varied. When the population of keys was small, the pianists could reach speeds of 7 keys/sec., with reasonably low rates of error. As the population increased, the speed of response dropped to around 4 keys/sec. Combining the number of keys and errors by calculating information transmitted, the experimenters found the maximum rate was about 22 bits/sec. This occurred for populations of from 15 to 37 keys. Larger and smaller alphabets gave lower rates. Similar experiments showed that the approximate maximum transmission rates for other skills were: typing, 17 bits/sec. (Quastler and Wulff, 1955); serial arithmetic, 23 bits/sec. (Quastler and Wulff, 1955); and reading familiar material, 40 bits/sec. (Pierce and Karlin, 1957). These values are all estimates from experiments using relatively well trained populations. It can be seen that most skilled tasks, using natural alphabets, have limits of fewer than 40 bits/sec. These limits represent practical maxima for familiar skills and provide a good way of comparing individual subjects and new methods of coding information against known standards.

SPEED VERSUS ACCURACY

Man has the ability to trade speed for accuracy. A typist may prepare a hurried rough draft in less time than it would take her to prepare a finished copy but it would contain more errors. A political speaker may impress his audience with the rapidity of his answers or he may take his time and prepare a more reasoned argument. In nearly every task, man can perform at varying levels of accuracy depending upon the rate at which he must act. This remarkable flexibility gives additional insight into the processes of skilled performance.

In the discussion concerning man's ability in simple RT, it was suggested that performance depends on the number of samples of information necessary for the subject to reach a given level of confidence about whether or not a signal had occurred. Now it is necessary to generalize that model to include tasks in which there are multiple stimuli. Here the major problem is not the intensity of the stimuli but the requirement that the subject discriminate between a variety of stimuli any one of which may occur on a given trial. Moreover, in this situation it is not possible to state in general what information the subject is actually using. In the simple RT situation it is clear that discrimination rests upon a detection of the difference in rate of internal activity. In choice RT, the information may be much more complex. For example, the subject may have to identify by their spatial location which of several lights have been lit up, or he may have to discriminate between two colors or two complex tonal patterns which form words, etc. Obviously it is not possible to generalize about the anatomical, physiological, or informational basis for such different discriminations, but it is possible to determine common characteristics of the sampling process used in making these decisions.

Implicit in the sampling model of this process is the notion that subjects can take additional samples of whatever information is relevant in order to determine which stimulus has occurred on a given trial. Since the information also contains noise, no one sample will allow perfect discrimination between the various stimuli. Rather, the probability of a correct response increases as the number of samples increases. If this notion is correct, it should be possible to vary the speed of the subject's response by encouraging him to take fewer samples. A detailed tradeoff between speed and accuracy could then be obtained.

An illustration of this tradeoff function in an actual experiment is provided by the following study (Fitts, 1966). Three groups of subjects performed the identical 16-choice RT task. They differed only in the incentive provided for their responses. The two experimental groups received, after each response, immediate augmented feedback about whether the response was right or wrong, fast or slow. Of these two groups, the speed group received extra points for making fast responses and relatively small penalties for errors. The accuracy group received a large penalty for an error and a relatively small bonus for being fast. The third (control) group was told to be as fast and accurate as possible and was given no augmented feedback.

The results of this study showed that the speed-group subjects were uniformly faster and made more errors than the accuracy group. The control group fell between the two others on both these measures. Two findings were of particular interest. First, the rate of information transmitted declined uniformly as errors increased beyond 10 per cent. That is, if the error rate went beyond 10 per cent, the increase in speed was not sufficient to compensate for the decrease in accuracy, and information transmitted declined. The data indicated that error rates of about 10 per cent gave the highest information transmission rate, with the rate of transmission declining if accuracy was either better or worse than this. This would mean that for *this* task optimum information transmission was attained at an error rate of about 10 per cent. Of course, not all tasks can tolerate such a high rate of error. The control group which was given ambiguous instructions and little feedback, performed at almost exactly the right error rate for maximal information transfer, 13 per cent. The accuracy group gave 10 per cent error and the highest transmission rate, while the speed group gave 22 per cent error and the lowest transmission rate. In this experiment the control subjects spontaneously selected an error rate close to the optimal.

The second interesting finding concerned the distribution of speeds for wrong responses. According to one sampling model, there should be nothing very special about an error. If the reaction-time situation can be described in terms of successive samples of information, then, for a given criterion, a certain proportion of error will result. When instructions place stress upon accuracy, RT is increased, allowing more samples to be taken and thus reducing the error. A sampling model suggests, therefore, that errors will have the same distribution of speeds as correct responses, since they are a natural and necessary consequence of the sampling process. In this study, the distribution of correct times and error times was virtually identical.

Much work needs to be done to extend to more tasks and to more payoff conditions this treatment of the speed-accuracy tradeoff. However, the fact that the rate of response which subjects adopted resulted in nearly optimal information transmission attests to the delicacy with which human processing capacities adjust to the environment. This finding corresponds qualitatively to everyday experience. In tasks like talking, writing, and typing we do not perform slowly enough to avoid all errors, but at a speed which will allow effective communication despite some error. Our language is well adapted to this compromise since it is highly redundant. That is, neither a misprint in typing nor a slip in speech will ordinarily make the utterance unintelligible. Rather, the receiver can use the redundancy of the language to correct the error.

In the discussion of the sampling model of choice RT it was suggested that the type of information which leads to a successful choice will differ greatly depending upon the coding of the stimulus information. This information may be auditory or visual, quantitative or qualitative. However, the model suggests that as the similarity among the stimulus alternatives increases, the amount of information that must be sampled for the subject to attain a given level of confidence must also increase. Crossman (1955) used cards with varying numbers of dots. The subjects were required to sort the cards into piles, each pile containing cards of the same number of dots. The discriminability between cards in the two piles was manipulated by varying the ratio of the number of dots on the cards assigned to the two piles. For example, if one pile contained cards with six dots and the other contained cards with three the ratio was 2:1, while if one pile had cards with three dots and the other with two, the ratio was 3:2. As the ratio declined so did the speed of sorting. This indicates that more sampling is required to reach a given level of accuracy when the discriminability is low than when it is high.

This section has suggested some factors which determine the rate at which the decision in choice RT is made. Each sample of incoming information provides evidence about which stimulus has occurred and, therefore, about which response is appropriate. As the number of samples increases, the accumulated evidence moves closer to the criterion level set by the subject. Since the information contains noise, there is a possibility that the decision will be in error, but this possibility decreases with the number of samples taken. The number of samples that the subject actually accumulates prior to the response depends upon the amount of evidence he needs to reach a given level of confidence. This number is greater for an infrequent signal than for a frequent signal since the *a priori* probability of an infrequent signal is small. The number of samples also increases as the signals become less discriminable and as the subject raises the criterion level required for a response. The criterion will vary with the reward for fast responses and the penalty for errors.

SERIAL AND CONTINUOUS PERFORMANCE

Skilled movements may be divided into two phases. The first phase involves the preparation for the movement while the second phase includes the movement to the goal. So far only the preparatory aspect of skills has been considered. The RT period allows the subject to prepare the subsequent motor responses. The preparation may be entirely covert, so that during the reaction-time period these processes must be inferred from actual performance. Or it may be overt— for example, the slight opening of a hand prior to its being closed around an object, a crouch before a jump. In this section, the movement portion of a simple skill will be considered. In subsequent sections the discussion will be expanded first to consideration of serial tasks and then to continuous tasks.

MOVEMENT TIME

The interrelation of response amplitude and accuracy is of obvious importance in determining the rate of movement. Older literature about this topic contains apparently contradictory findings as to the relation between amplitude and movement time. In one set of studies, investigators found that the time for a movement is almost completely independent of amplitude. This is true, for example, if you move your hand back and forth as rapidly as possible, and it is also true for handwriting (Freeman, 1914). Have someone time you while you write your name (writing as fast as you can for, say fifteen seconds), first in a relatively large script, then in a small script. You will find that the number of letters you can write will not vary more than 2 per cent or 3 per cent irrespective, within wide limits, of the size of your writing. Other studies, however, particularly studies made during World War II, in connection with the design of control devices, have found that large movements took much longer to execute than small movements where both had to be terminated with equal precision. The answer to these apparently discrepant findings is that if *relative* accuracy is the major consideration, or if accuracy of terminating the movement is unimportant, then increasing movement amplitude does not affect movement time, but if *absolute* precision is required in terminating the movement, then the larger the movement the slower will be its completion. The use of information measures provides a precise way to specify these relationships.

INFORMATION CAPACITY OF THE MOTOR SYSTEM

In 1953 and 1954, shortly after psychologists first began to see some of the opportunities for applying information theory to the study of human performance, a way was proposed (Fitts, 1954) of specifying the difficulty of motor tasks. This method has turned out to be useful for predicting the time required for a great variety of motor responses. The measure is based on the ratio of accuracy to amplitude, and thus resembles the Weber ratio in sensory psychophysics (see page 46), although, as is customary with information measures, the logarithm to the base 2 of this ratio is employed. Thus, the *ID* (index of movement difficulty) is defined as:

$$ID = \log_2 2A/W \qquad (1)$$

where A is the amplitude of movement and W is the total tolerance for error in terminating the movement. The value of W is equivalent to the size of a bull's eye in rifle shooting, for example. If one thinks of aiming directly at the bull's eye, the maximum error which is possible if one is to hit it is, of course, the radius, or one-half the diameter. Thus, in computing the ratio of amplitude to error, one-half W is used; which gives the fraction:

$$A/\tfrac{1}{2}W \quad \text{or} \qquad (2)$$
$$2A/W \qquad (3)$$

Taking the logarithm to the base 2 of this fraction is equivalent to asking how much information is generated by the selection of a given movement out of $2A/W$-possible-movements of that accuracy. In order to make this index of task difficulty meaningful, consider the following examples:

Suppose that an individual has to move his pencil a distance of 8 inches and then place a dot in a circle ¼ inch in diameter. The index of difficulty in this case would be

$$ID = \log_2 (2 \times 8/\tfrac{1}{4}) = \log_2 64 = 6 \text{ bits} \qquad (4)$$

Results have shown that a movement of this degree of difficulty requires of the average person about ½ second. Two such movements per second would enable the person to produce twelve bits of response information per second, which is about the limit of the response system for tasks of this type. Movements which generate only 3 bits of information can be performed at about 4 per second. For example, a movement of 4 inches executed with a tolerance of 1 inch permits an individual to make approximately four movements per second.

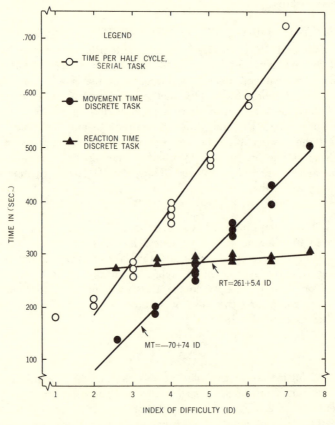

Figure 33

Reaction time and movement time in the execution of tasks which vary in amplitude and accuracy (ID). The open circles are movement times in a serial task, the filled circles are movement times in a discrete task, and the triangles are reaction times for the discrete task. (After Fitts and Peterson, 1964.)

A formal experiment conducted in 1964 (Fitts and Peterson) confirms these predictions and illustrates the relationship between two aspects of a skilled movement. In this experiment the subject had to move a stylus a variable distance, in the direction indicated by a light. The movement was to terminate in a slit, the size of which could be varied. The independent variables were the number of directions (1 or 2) and the index of difficulty, obtained by equation 1 from the amplitude of movement and the size of the slit. With two directions, the subject did not know whether he was to move left or right until the light came on. He then moved as rapidly as possible from the home button to the slit in the direction indicated by the light. The dependent variables were the time between the onset of the direction light and the subject lifting his stylus off the home button (reaction time) and the time from the start of the movement until its termination (movement time). Figure 33 shows these two times as a function of the index of difficulty. Notice that increasing the difficulty index has a great effect on movement time but almost none on reaction time. On the other hand, increasing the number of directions from 1 to 2—that is, adding 1 bit of directional information—increases the reaction time but not the movement time. This experiment shows that both times are under the control of aspects of the experimental situation but that they are quite separate. Reaction time reflects the subject's uncertainty about which of a set of movements is to occur, while movement time reflects the relative accuracy of termination required by the movement.

The reciprocal of the slope of the linear relation between movement time and index of difficulty represents the rate of information transmission in this task. The maximum rate here is about 12 bits per second. The rate of information is, as predicted, relatively constant over the values of ID. This value represents a capacity for the motor system in this type of simple, one-dimensional movement but should not be thought of as a limit for all motor tasks. Just as in absolute judgment, the capacity can be raised if the number of response dimensions is increased. While there is no theoretical limit, holding across all tasks, to the rate at which information can be transmitted, the relatively fixed capacity for one-dimensional movements and the separate effects of uncertainty on reaction and movement time are important findings in an effort to quantify movement elements.

SERIAL TASKS

The data considered in the last section involve movements which require from .1 to .5 seconds from initiation to completion. Since it has been shown that it requires about .3 seconds (Hick, 1948) for feedback from the muscles to affect the aiming of a skilled movement, only the most difficult of the movements could have been affected by feedback, and even here the correction would have to be initiated at the very start of the movement. These movements are essentially pre-programmed and involve little or no correction from intrinsic visual and kinesthetic feedback once they are initiated. Of course, the augmented feedback from the experimenter after completion of the movement has its effect upon the *next* response.

It is possible now to extend our analysis to serial tasks; that is, tasks which involve a series of movements. In these tasks, the rigid separation between reaction time and movement time is lost, and several important properties of more complicated skills are allowed to emerge. First, feedback information from previous responses is received and presumably processed by the subject during the task. Second, the subject may be allowed to preview future stimuli during his response to prior stimuli. In many skills, such as reading aloud, the motor response greatly lags behind the intake of stimulus information. Serial tasks allow the study of such preview and anticipation. Finally, these tasks allow the subject to pace his performance. His ability to adjust performance to the assimilation of advanced information and feedback involves several of the limitations discussed in Chapter 4.

The discrete-movement tasks discussed in the previous section have also been studied in a serial form (Fitts, 1954). In this situation, the subject moved back and forth between targets. The size of the target and amplitude of the movement were varied in different conditions. The study summarized performance in terms of mean movement time as a function of the index of difficulty. The results are plotted in the upper line of Figure 33. The times for the serial task represent the average length of time to move between the two targets and do not separate between reaction and movement time. The overall times in the serial task are about .1 to .2 seconds longer than the movement times in the discrete task. This value is not as great as the typical reaction time in the discrete situation (.3 sec.). While the processing of feedback information from the movement increases the average time per movement by about .1 to .2 seconds, the fact that this is shorter than the typical reaction time suggests that the processing of feedback data can, to some extent, overlap the planning and execution of other movements. The addition of feedback information slows the movement, but not as much as it would if the subject had to cease responding completely while it was being processed.

If the processing of feedback from prior movements can overlap with present responses it is also reasonable to expect some advanced processing of available information concerning future stimuli. In fact,

this is known to be the case. When we read aloud our eyes lead our voice by several words, so that if the page were suddenly to go blank we might read for a short while from memory. The skilled pianist is ready to turn the page well before his fingers have played the last note on the page. Such preview or anticipation is what makes the analysis of serial tasks so much more complicated than the analysis of discrete tasks. It is impossible to know exactly what information is being processed at a given moment. However, knowledge of the component functions allows a number of predictions to be checked in the serial situation. These are as follows:

1. Information about future stimuli will aid performance, but only up, to the limit of man's ability to process such information. Thus, as the uncertainty of the present response or future stimuli increases the ability of man to utilize preview information is reduced.

2. As the time between the reception of new information and its use increases, memory will play a more important role, and advance information will become of less advantage due to loss from short-term memory.

3. As the task continues, the tendency to switch sensory channels will lead to occasional interruptions in the processing, showing up in increased times.

All of these suggestions have received substantial confirmation in the study of serial tasks. Unfortunately, not enough work has been done with any one task situation to make a quantitative specification of these processes.

CONTINUOUS TASKS

Continuous tasks are those in which the stimulus input is continuously changing. For example, in driving, the position of the car with respect to the road is changing continuously in time, as is the position of a duck being tracked by a hunter. Can results which have been obtained from discrete and serial cases be applied to continuous cases? If the analysis of human-performance limitations outlined in Chapter is correct, it is not possible for man to make corrections in his response on a continuous basis. Thus, while the input of a task may be a continuously changing function, the output cannot be. In this section evidence for such an assertion will be explored.

It is necessary to point out that even if man is unable continuous adjustments in tracking a course, this inability prevent him from successfully following a predictable course hunter can anticipate the rate and course of the duck and it successfully as long as it remains regular. The role of

has previously been discussed in connection with simple RT tasks, where it was shown that the delay in response could be reduced to nearly zero if the time of the signal was completely predictable. Evidence on the ability of man to make continuous corrections must come from tracking of irregular and unpredictable inputs so that anticipation is reduced.

The first writer to suggest that man was discontinuous in making corrections in a tracking task was Craik (1948). He observed that corrections in the subject's response did not occur more frequently than twice a second. Craik suggested that these discrete corrections were a consequence of the psychological refractory period. The refractory period refers to the delay in handling the second of two closely spaced signals (p. 79). In a continuous course, Craik suggested that this limitation in man's processing rate prevented him from handling more than two error corrections during a second.

Because one cannot be certain from an interpretation of tracking records that corrections by the operator are not continuous, Craik's hypothesis has been tested in a less direct way.

According to the mathematical theory of waveform description, it is necessary to sample only twice as often as the highest frequency present in the waveform to describe it completely. Thus, in a simple tracking task two samples per cycle might be thought of as the minimum rate at which man could sample and track accurately. In actual practice man seems to require more information than this minimum. For example, according to Birmingham and Taylor (1954), "practical experience indicates that at least four samples per cycle are required to reproduce the waveform of the input (in tracking) with reasonable fidelity." Empirical studies which blank out the course for varying periods (Poulton, 1950) have confirmed the reasonableness of this estimate. If the rate at which man must sample is taken at between 2 and 4 samples per cycle and if Craik is also right in suggesting that man is able to make only two error corrections per second, then it is possible to predict the maximum course frequency which man can track effectively (Pew, 1965). This prediction is obtained by dividing the number of samples or corrections which man can make per second (2) by the number of samples per cycle required to reproduce the waveform (2 to 4). The value is approximately .5 to 1 cycle per second. Elkind and Sprague (1961) provide data on a tracking task, which can be used to test these assumptions. In their study the maximum frequency ($f$co) of the input was varied. Figure 34 shows the effect of varying the input frequency upon the rate of information transmission in two different types of tracking. The data indicate that information transmission improves regularly until just about .5 to 1 cycle per second. After

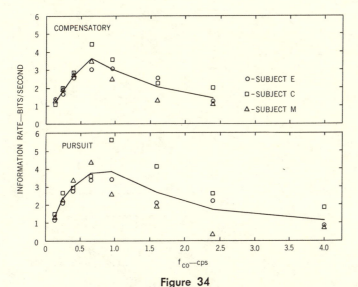

Figure 34

*Information transmission rates for two tracking
tasks as a function of the maximum frequency
(fco) of the input function, measured in cycles
per second. (After Elkind and Sprague, IRE
Transactions on Human Factors in Electronics,
1961.)*

this value is reached, errors begin to rise rapidly˙and the information
rate drops. The data provide nice support for the assumptions suggested above. Of course, they do not prove that the assumptions are
correct; however, they are consistent with the view being expressed
in this section.

A number of other studies have applied an informational analysis
to continuous tasks. The findings have supported the general limitations that have been discussed under the heading of discrete and
serial processing. Crossman (1960a) varied the rate of input information in a tracking task that required the subject to follow a changing
course. The results for his four skilled subjects are shown in Figure 35.
The upper graph depicts a condition in which there is no preview.
Notice that the information-transmission rates for all subjects are limited to about 5 bits per second. Regardless of the information in the
input, subjects never transmit more than this value. The use of preview
in conditions represented in the lower graph allows the subjects to
obtain advanced information about future changes in the course. Preview increases the rate of information transmission for all subjects.

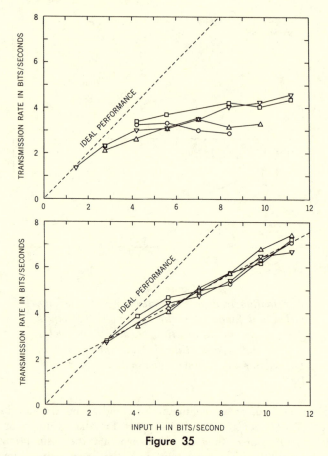

Figure 35

Transmission rates in bits per second for track-
ing tasks as a function of the input information.
The upper set of curves represents a task with-
out preview, while the lower set represents a
task with preview. The individual curves repre-
sent the data from different subjects. (Adapted
from Crossman, 1960.)

This is in accord with the view that information about future responses
can overlap with present processing. Moreover, in the preview condition there is no clear evidence for a limit to the rate of transmission, although this experiment did not carry the analysis sufficiently
far to determine whether or where that limit exists. Crossman specu-
lates that the limit, with preview, will be 10 bits/sec., which is

about the maximum in the linear-movement tasks (see pp. 113–115).

These data reveal that continuous tasks can be analyzed using some of the same tools which have been applied to discrete and serial tasks. These results also indicate the utility of an informational analysis for many types of perceptual-motor skills.

SUMMARY

In this chapter a detailed analysis of many aspects of skilled performance has been attempted. The analysis began with simple RT tasks. It was shown how the addition of temporal and event uncertainty increased RT by increasing the demands to search among alternatives and sustain attention. Moreover, the effect of uncertainty was shown not to be a fixed and unvarying one, but to reflect delicately the state of training and compatibility of the S-R code.

Reaction-time tasks were viewed as involving a decision based on successive samples of sensory information. Each sample provides noisy data with respect to the stimuli. The longer the subject samples, the fewer errors he will make, but the longer will be his response time. The number of samples taken is governed by aspects of the task, including rewards, costs, and special instructions.

Skills involve both a preparation and a movement. It was shown that reaction time and movement time are controlled by separate aspects of the task requirements. Movement time is a linear function of the information generated by the movement. In this way, each component of skill may be viewed as containing a preparatory period and a period of execution, each with its own empirical laws.

The next step in the argument was to combine sequences of movements in a serial task. These tasks reveal new aspects of man's skilled performance. First, processing of feedback information reduces the rate of a movement but, by overlapping with the movement itself, reduces it less than the full reaction time. Second, preview allows processing of future responses during the performance of present responses. The effectiveness of preview depends upon the total amount of information to be processed and the load placed upon memory by the storage of the preview information.

Finally, tasks with continuous input were considered. Evidence suggests, although it hardly proves, that man responds discontinuously. The frequency of his response is limited by the time required to collect samples of information from the environment. After each sample he can correct discrepancies between his position and the course. These corrections seem to be limited to about two per second, as is suggested by the psychological refractory period. It is possible to analyze continuous skills in terms of information transmission rates.

The results of the chapter demonstrate that complex human skills may be fruitfully studied through an analysis of the components, which involve different information-processing functions.

Most psychologists believe that complex functions, such as those involved in language and problem solving, are based upon and arise out of simpler skills. Sir Frederick Bartlett (1958, pp. 11-12) has outlined the close relation of thinking to perceptual-motor skills: *

It seems reasonable to try to begin by treating thinking provisionally as a complex and high-level kind of skill. Thinking has its acknowledged experts, like every other known form of skill and in both cases much of the expertness, though never, perhaps, all of it, has to be acquired by well-informed practice. Every kind of bodily skill is based upon evidence picked up directly or indirectly from the environment, and used for the attempted achievement of whatever issue may be required at the time of the performance. Every kind of thinking also claims that it is based upon information or evidence which, again, must be picked up directly or indirectly from the environment and which is used in an attempt to satisfy some requirement of the occasion upon which the thinking takes place.

This chapter will be concerned primarily with an analysis of complex skills involving what may be called higher mental functions—for example, thinking and problem solving, which depend at least in part upon language. Language skills will be studied through an analysis of their component functions, in much the same way as has been done for perceptual-motor skills.

Language skills are ordinarily thought to be especially complex forms of behavior. This statement needs considerable clarification in the light of the obvious fact that perceptual-motor skills are also complex. It may be just as difficult to program a computer to hit a baseball or to play tennis as it is to program it to play chess. The view of reaction time as a serial decision process requires that the mechanisms responsible for such a skill be sophisticated. The major reason that language skills appear to be more complex than perceptual-motor skills is the overwhelming richness of alternative situations where language is employed.

Consider the process of multiplication. As children we learn the multiplication tables so well that when we are asked to multiply 6

*From F. C. Bartlett, *Thinking*, New York: Basic Books, 1958. Reprinted by permission of George Allen & Unwin, Ltd.

times 7, the answer comes quite automatically. Automatic means that we are unaware of the search process involved in arriving at the answer. In this respect it is much like hitting a baseball, where we are also unaware of the selection of the appropriately timed response from the different muscular sequences which are possible. However, once the multiplication problem goes much beyond 12 times 12, the process becomes different. It is not possible to have an automated answer to all multiplication problems. Therefore, multiplication of higher numbers involves the systematic application of a simple rule. We are well aware of the processes which lie behind the formation and application of the rule, and it now appears appropriate to say we actively sought a solution to the problem.

Man's ability to recognize words when spoken by many different voices or written in different prints was discussed earlier. These are examples of language skills which have been practiced and have reached high levels of automation. In common usage, these tasks are not thought to involve higher mental processes, or thinking. They can be contrasted with a problem-solving task. Once the problem has been solved, practice is rarely continued. No doubt many very complex problems, like proving theorems in logic or mathematics, could become highly routine and automated if practice was continued on a single problem.

In the study of perceptual-motor skills, emphasis was placed on the rate of transmission of information because in most of these skills speed is important. Many language skills, particularly problem solving, are concerned more with success than with speed. In what follows, an attempt will be made to adapt the approach taken so far to this special characteristic of language skills.

TRANSFORMATIONS

All skills involve the presentation of information from the environment. They also demand that this information be returned to the environment in the form of a response. This section analyzes the ways in which such transfer of information takes place.

CONSERVATION

Nearly all of the tasks which have been considered in earlier chapters require the subject to conserve information if he is to accomplish the task. For example, in the choice reaction-time task the subject is required to effect a change in energy and location, but he must preserve all the information. He may convert a light to a key press, or a printed word to a spoken word, but for each stimulus there is a proper response. If the performance is without error, it is always possible for the observer who watches the responses to recover the sequence of stimuli. The same is true in the absolute-judgment task. The subject is required to discriminate by providing each stimulus with a unique response. The properties of conserving tasks are schematized at the left part of Figure 36.

Such tasks have been examined in some detail over the course of the last several chapters. It was pointed out that reaction time increases

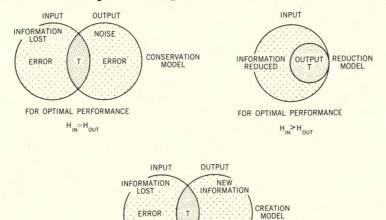

Figure 36

Three different types of information-processing tasks are illustrated. In each diagram the relationship between stimulus and response information is different. (After Posner, 1964.)

with the amount of information transmitted. However, with a constant amount of information transmitted per response there are still differences—these depend upon the stimulus and response codes—in the time taken to respond. If the process relating stimulus code to response code is called a *transformation,* then the difficulty of a transformation may be measured by the time it takes to perform it. It has already been suggested that reaction time varies with the degree of compatibility between stimulus and response codes. Thus, for conservation tasks the more compatible the S-R codes, as measured by population stereotypes, the simpler the transformation process. It has also been found that compatible S-R codes with simple transformation can be auto-mated more quickly than less compatible tasks. These tasks require less of the subject's limited capacity and interfere less with other tasks.

REDUCTION

Pattern recognition is an example of a perceptual-motor skill which does not involve information conservation. If "A" and "a" are translated by the same name, more than one stimulus is mapped into the same response. In classification the subject is not required to pre-serve all the information in the stimulus.

Tasks of this type are frequent in man's behavior, particularly in language skills. A number of noted psychologists have pointed this out. Attneave (1963, p. 634), for example, says, "Most of the information that goes into the individual never comes out again. The information that is lost is not necessarily wasted, however. The situation is some-what like that of an executive who considers a mountain of data . . . in order to arrive at a one-bit decision."

These tasks are called *information reducing*. They require that the subject map more than one stimulus into a single response. All classi-fication tasks, including pattern recognition and the learning of con-cepts, are examples. Adding numbers is also a good example. The sum of a set of numbers contains less information than the numbers them-selves. It is not possible to recover the original numbers from their sum, since more than one set will give the same result. In losing informa-tion about the original numbers, however, the subject has not made an error but, rather, has accomplished his task. For information-reduc-tion tasks, therefore, loss of information is not necessarily error, but may be required to accomplish the task. The top right diagram in Fig-ure 36 schematizes the information-reduction task.

The *size of the transformation* relating input and output can be measured for reduction tasks. The input and output information are clearly different in these tasks, and the difference represents the sub-ject's contribution in condensing the information. It might be hypothe-sized that performance in such tasks is a function of the amount of information which is reduced between input and output (transforma-tion size). In order to test this hypothesis it is necessary to hold constant the degree of learning, compatibility, memory, and other factors.

Before testing of this hypothesis, it is necessary to make a distinc-tion between two types of information reduction. Consider a task in which you are required to classify books by their color. In such a task you can ignore size, shape, and content. Such a task clearly involves information reduction, but the emphasis is placed on selection. An infor-mation-reduction task that requires selection—that is, allows aspects of the stimulus to be ignored—will be called a *gating task*. On the other hand, consider the classification of digits into odd or even. What aspect of the digit can be ignored in making such a classification? None at all. The entire digit must be processed and then classified into either of two categories. The response "odd" does not conserve the stimulus information, but rather represents it in a reduced or condensed form. Information-reduction tasks of this type are called *condensation tasks*.

A number of studies have been concerned with the subject's ability to learn rules of classification. These have been called concept-learning studies. Concept learning may involve either gating or condensation or both. A concept task which involves only gating is shown in the left box (I) of Figure 37. These eight figures differ along three dimen-

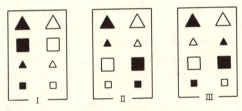

Figure 37

Three different methods of classifying eight stimuli into two categories. The stimuli vary on three dimensions: size, color, and shape. The methods have one, two, or three dimensions relevant to the classification. (Adapted from Shepard, Hovland, and Jenkins, 1961.)

sions: size, shape, and color. Since there are two values of each dimension, there are 3 bits of stimulus information. Suppose the subject is required to learn to classify these patterns into two categories. Let us call the stimuli in the left column of box I positive and those in the right column negative. The stimuli are presented in random order. The subject has to learn which stimuli are positive and which are negative. Notice that the only aspect of the stimuli to which the subject must attend in order to make this classification is the color; he can ignore both shape and size. In a typical learning experiment the subject sees one stimulus at a time and is told whether it is positive or negative. He must learn to attend only to the color dimension in order to perform the classification. Experiments of this type have shown that the speed of learning is inversely related to the number of irrelevant dimensions. That is, the more information the subject must learn to ignore, the slower he learns.

In general, once the subject has learned the rule in a gating task, he has little trouble in ignoring large amounts of information. It is easy to attend just to the color. The process of selection can be automated, and it then becomes independent of the amount of irrelevant information. This generalization depends upon two conditions. First, the source of relevant information must be stable so that the task does not require searching. Search tasks depend upon the number of items through which the subject scans (see Chapter 4). Second, the code used must allow easy separation of the relevant from the irrelevant information. Suppose you are required to classify words written in different colors of ink. It would be easy to ignore the word and attend only to the ink unless the word happened to be a color name. Learning to classify the word red written in green has proved to be difficult. However, except in the case of such highly incompatible codes, most gating tasks, once the rule is known, can be performed with efficiency as high as if the irrelevant information were not present.

The story is somewhat different with condensation tasks. Consider the right box (III) of Figure 37. In this case, the same eight stimuli are divided into two classes, but the information is distributed in such a way that all three dimensions (color, size, shape) must be processed in order to classify each instance. None of the information can be ignored in making a response. This is clearly a condensation task. Condensation tasks are like gating tasks in that the addition of information results in an increase in the time necessary to learn the classification. In general, the rate of increase of difficulty with increasing information is greater in a condensation task than in a similar gating task. The middle box (II) requires some condensation and some gating, since two dimensions are relevant (shape and color) and one can be ignored (size).

Performance of already learned classification rules differs according to whether condensation or gating is required. Consider three tasks, all of which involve the transmission of one bit of information. The first requires the subject to push one button when a circle appears and another when a square appears. There is no irrelevant information. This is a standard information-conserving reaction-time task. In condition two, the subject is required to classify patterns: one circle, two circles, one square and two squares. The first two require pressing the left key and the last two the right key. This is an information-reduction task which allows gating since the number may be ignored. In condition three the same stimuli are used as in the last condition, but one circle and two squares require the left key and two circles and one square require the right key. The results of a study involving these three tasks (Fitts and Biederman, 1965) indicate that the gating task quickly reached the same level of performance as the conservation task but the condensation task took longer, even after considerable practice. In fact, the condensation task took about as long as if the subject had four separate responses to make.

This result also holds for other types of condensation tasks. It takes longer to classify a digit into odd or even, which represents only 1 bit transmitted, than to name the digit, which transmits 3.3 bits, although both tasks are highly practiced.

These examples indicate that information-reduction tasks do not increase in difficulty as the amount of information transmitted increases. Rather, their difficulty depends much more upon the difference between input and output information or upon the amount of information that is reduced.

One study of condensation (Posner, 1964b) has produced quantitative relationships between the amount of information reduction which the tasks required and the subject's performance. In this experiment the stimulus information always consisted of sets of eight numbers selected randomly from 1 to 64. The numbers were presented to the subjects over earphones. The subjects were required either to record the numbers or operate upon them by a variety of information-reducing transformations. The tasks were the following: (1) record, which involved writing down the numbers; (2) record-sum, in which recording alternated with adding together the digits of a given number—for example, 57 was transformed into 12; (3) partial addition, in which successive pairs of numbers were added; (4) 2-bit classification, which involved placing each number into one of four categories: high-odd, high-even, low-odd, low-even; (5) 1-bit classification, in which high and odd or low and even constituted one category while the reverse constituted the other; and finally (6), complete addition, in which all the numbers were added to produce a single sum. The tasks were chosen so that the output information varied from 7.7 to 48 bits and so that the component operations were relatively familiar. It was not possible to compare the tasks directly because errors were defined differently for each task. Therefore, the rate at which errors increased was measured for each task as it was speeded. The basic notion was that the more difficult the task or the more processing the transformation required, the greater would be the loss in performance as the task was speeded.

The results of this study confirmed the notion that task difficulty increased as the amount of information reduction increased. For this set of tasks and under the conditions outlined in this experiment, the relation between the amount of information reduced and the percentage of increase in error with speeding was approximately linear. This finding must be carefully qualified since the tasks used here were not equally familiar and, therefore, were difficult to compare. It does however, lend encouragement to the hypothesis that the difficulty of a transformation in a condensation task is a function of the information reduced. The amount of information reduction in a condensation task plays very much the same role as the degree of compatibility in a conservation task. Both represent efforts to describe the difficulty of the transformations which intervene between stimulus and response.

CREATION

The final logical category of transformations upon input information is shown in the bottom part of Figure 36. In this kind of task the subject is required to create or elaborate upon the information presented in the input. The importance in human behavior of elaboration upon input is very great. Jerome Bruner (1957, p. 41) has suggested that, "the most characteristic thing about mental life is that one constantly goes beyond the information given." However, even though one does go beyond the information given, the label *information creation* is somewhat misleading. The elaboration that takes place is based in part on information which the subject has learned previously. That is, information creation places great stress upon the subject's memory.

Consider, for example, the free-association experiment. The subject is provided with a word and asked to give as many responses as he can in a fixed time. If no context is provided, the subject is perfectly free to generate information. In one such experiment (Shepard, 1963), subjects were able to produce about 20 words a minute for five minutes. The first minute showed a slightly higher rate than subsequent minutes. When constraint was introduced in the form of a context into which the words had to fit, the rate of production declined rapidly. With one context word the rate dropped by a third, and with forty words of context it was about one-tenth of the no-context value. The theoretical limit is when the context is so great that only one answer is correct. For example: "Give the opposite of 'up'." In this case we have an information-conserving or translation situation.

The Shepard data deal with a situation in which the subject is free to create as many responses as he can. In this situation, as the uncertainty about the response is increased by elimination of context, the rate of production of items improves. This is the opposite of what happens to the rate of response when stimulus uncertainty is increased in a conservation task. Performance in this type of information creation is an increasing function of uncertainty.

As was suggested in Chapter 1, "information creation" should not be confused with "creativity." Creativity depends upon more than the production or elaboration of responses. It also depends upon the selection of appropriate choices from among those responses. Consider the task of producing a word in a normal sentence. As the context increases, the amount of uncertainty concerning the appropriate word decreases. It has been shown (Goldman-Eisler, 1958) that pauses which occur in human speech are associated with positions of high uncertainty. That is, speech is slowed and hesitation occurs when the subject has great choice about which word should be inserted. While information creation is speeded as constraint is removed, information selection (which involves reduction) becomes increasingly difficult as uncertainty is increased. Most creative acts must involve both generation and selection. They, therefore, combine two types of transformation, which are quite differently affected by the total uncertainty.

Unfortunately, the experimental and quantitative analysis of tasks which involve information creation is not well developed. Much less is known about these tasks than about either conservation or reduction tasks. Nonetheless, it is possible to investigate the component aspects of creativity—that is, information creation and selection; and future research may help to clarify these tasks. It should be pointed out that creativity must involve many of the same component functions and limitations in information processing as other complex tasks.

In summary, language skills may be seen as involving three fundamental types of information transformation. The first, information conservation, is by far the most thoroughly explored since it is frequently involved in perceptual-motor skills as well as in language skills. The second, information reduction, is less well understood, but experiments have provided some support for the proposition that the difficulty of such transformation is a function of the amount of information reduction. Finally, information creation is poorly understood, although it appears that performance improves with increased uncertainty in this task. In addition, information creation must involve previous learning and memory in an important way. It will now be possible to consider evidence with respect to human limitations in making these transformations.

THE SINGLE-CHANNEL HYPOTHESIS

At several points this book has suggested a view of man as a single processing channel limited in its ability to process events. In Chapter 4 it was shown that even though man does have limits to his processing capacity, he is by no means limited to processing a single event. Rather, the extent of his limitation is, in part, a function of the uncertainty of the signals. As temporal and event uncertainty increases, the decline in efficiency in the performance of one task due to the addition of another is magnified. Thus, the idea of man as a processing channel limited for information rather than for events *per se* was introduced. But this characterization was also incomplete. The incompleteness was illustrated in Chapter 6, as experiments were introduced which demonstrated that there is no theoretical upper limit for the transmission of information in perceptual-motor skills, providing that the tasks are highly overlearned and compatible. Nonetheless, important practical limits could be stated in specific situations. Examples of these are absolute judgment, accuracy of motor responses, and discrete processing tasks using familiar codes like piano keys, typewriter keys, and common English words.

It is now time to take another step in modifying the idea of man as a single processing channel. Like previous suggestions, this modification is unlikely to be the final one or to fit all situations, but it proves fruitful in many language skills. *The limitation in central processing capacity depends upon the size of the transformation that is required between stimulus and response or between stimulus and memory.* The greater the size of the transformation, the more the interference between two tasks.

The definition of the size of a transformation depends upon the type of task in which the subject is engaged. In a conservation task, the transformation size varies with the degree of compatibility, while in a reduction task it depends upon the amount of information reduced. No general measure is yet available for creation tasks. According to this view, the degree to which two signals can be successfully processed simultaneously depends upon both the uncertainty of the signal and the size of the transformation between input and output.

Broadbent (1964) lent support to this latter point for conservation tasks. He used two levels of compatibility. The compatible condition involved pressing down upon a vibrating key, while the incompatible condition required the subject to press the same finger of the hand opposite the vibrating key. These tasks differed, as would be expected, both in RT and in the rate of information transmitted. Moreover, the incompatible task caused a more severe decrement in performance upon a simultaneous auditory task than did the compatible RT task. In addition, studies have shown that practice on one skilled task will reduce its effect upon performance in a simultaneous activity (Bahrick, Noble, and Fitts, 1954). Since the amount of practice is one source of compatibility, this finding agrees with the general principle discussed above.

Additional evidence for the utility of the notion of man as a channel limited in its capacity for transformation comes from tasks which involve short-term memory. This evidence is particularly crucial because virtually all language skills involve a combination of retention of prior information with transformation of incoming input.

MEMORY AND TRANSFORMATION

Few experiments, even among those normally called "memory tasks," find man storing untransformed stimulus information. Rather, man uses his past experience and his knowledge about the type of response he will have to make to transform the input in a way which will reduce his storage load. If the experimenter is interested primarily in memory, he does everything possible to reduce these transformations. Thus, he uses ordered recall, which forces the conservation of input information, presents difficult-to-organize strings of unrelated items such as nonsense syllables and figures, gives different material to several sensory channels simultaneously, or attempts to block the central processing capacity of the subject with other tasks.

The way in which a transformation can improve retention is illustrated by a study of memory span (Miller, 1956). Normally, the memory span for binary numbers is only slightly larger than for decimal numbers; i.e., about twelve items. However, one subject was taught to recode the binary digits into decimal digits. The recoding is relatively simple. For every three binary numbers a single digit is assigned. For example, the binary digits 000 are coded as 0 while the digits 111 are coded as 7. By this technique the size of the memory span was tripled. However, such transformations are not without a penalty. The memory span is only slightly affected by an increase in the rate of presentation of the items. When a transformation of this type is required, the rate of presentation becomes critical. It takes time to translate the binary digits into a new code, just as any transformation of stimulus input takes time. In this case, provided that the rate of receiving information is low, the time is worth while; but if the rate is high, the number of items retained might well be below the normal binary span.

Since most language skills involve both transformation and memory, the relation between the two is of critical importance. In the previous study, it was shown how relatively simple transformations can improve retention. In most tasks such transformations are necessary. The use of an outline to record a lecture represents a kind of classification of the stimulus; it is a transformation like those discussed under the heading of information reduction. Even with a pencil and paper to aid memory, verbatim transcription is rarely possible. In fact, the value of an outline depends on how much the transformations involve condensation rather than gating of information. Such transformations are absolutely necessary. The limitations of human memory are too great to allow storage of much untransformed information.

Is it possible to specify the interaction between these two processes in any exact way? The answer seems to lie in another extension of the single-channel idea, an extension which is confirmed by the experimentation outlined below. Heretofore, man has been seen as limited in the processing of input information, the limitation being both for the amount of information and the size of the transformation involved. Now it is suggested that the information which is in short-term storage also competes for this limited capacity. The idea is easy to conceive. Suppose you have just looked up a telephone number. If nothing interrupts you, there is a high probability that you will retain it long enough to dial. However, if you are distracted, this probability drops. "Distracted" may be interpreted as meaning that a part of your attention has been commanded by the processing of some other stimulus. In the previous section, it was shown that attention is not an all-or-none matter, but depends upon the amount of the limited processing capacity or single channel which is used. Thus, increases in the size of a transformation should cause a corresponding loss in the information stored in short-term memory. In fact, in Chapter 4, short-term memory was defined as a system which loses information in the absence of continued attention.

Two series of experiments have tested the validity of this general idea. Crowder (1964) had subjects retain strings of five unrelated nouns during a subsequent serial key-press task. The key-press task began immediately after the five words had been presented and it continued for 24 seconds. Afterwards, the subjects attempted to recall the words in the order in which they had been presented. The key-press task was a standard serial reaction-time situation in which each press turned off a light and presented the next stimulus. The results showed that the key-press task significantly reduced retention and that a low-compatibility S-R arrangement had more effect than a high-compatibility arrangement. In addition, practice helped to reduce the effectiveness of the key-press task in causing forgetting. This is direct confirmation of the notion that the channel handles both incoming and stored information and that it is affected by the size of the transformation.

Another series of studies (Posner and Rossman, 1965) extended the notion to information-reducing transformations. The stored material consisted of three-digit numbers. The interpolated tasks involved self-paced transformations upon two-digit numbers, varying in amount of information reduction (see page 129). The interpolated stimuli were the same for all tasks. Since the task was self-paced, however, the number of items interpolated declined as the transformation size increased. The results, in terms of percentage of errors of the three-digit numbers, are shown in Figure 38 as a function of time in store

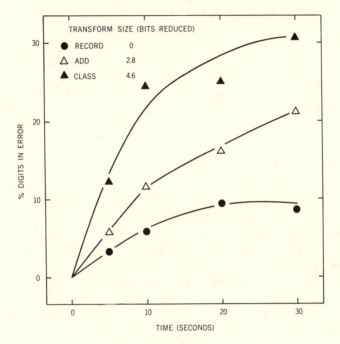

Figure 38

Errors in retention as a function of time between presentation and recall for interpolated tasks differing in the size of the transformation. (Adapted from Posner and Rossman, 1965.)

for three different levels of information reduction. Notice that forgetting is very slight if the interpolated task involves only the recording of digits, while it is severe if the interpolated task requires classification. In general, the rate of forgetting is an increasing function of the size of the transformation. This same general finding holds with a variety of types of stored material.

CONCLUSION

Language skills involve both memory and transformation. The single-channel hypothesis suggests how these processes interact in human information processing. In short, man is viewed as a single channel limited in the amount of information that can be processed simultaneously. This limitation involves not only the information transmission rate, but also the size of the transformations involved in producing the output from the input information. Both incoming stimuli and information stored in short-term memory compete for the limited capacity.

This view of man can be used to shed light on many tasks which begin to approach those of everyday life. In no sense can complete or rigorous predictions be made concerning these tasks. However, important aspects of such human activities as reading and listening can be viewed in these terms. This chapter lays the groundwork for a more advanced study of these situations.

READING AND LISTENING

One way of summarizing the analysis presented so far is to describe it as a study of the interaction of memory and thought. Incompatible information-conserving transformations such as solving anagrams and cracking codes, and information-reducing transformations, such as addition and classification are aspects of thinking. They do not capture the concept of thinking in all the ways in which it is used in everyday language. They are most congruent with the type of thinking which is involved in the solution of problems, or what Bartlett (1959) called "real hard thinking." However, they have the advantage of being defined in a more complete and rigorous way than the everyday usages of the term can be, and they allow the experimental investigation of those aspects of thinking with which they are concerned.

The most common forms in which adults use language are the tasks of reading, listening, and speaking. These are all good examples of the close relation between perceptual-motor and language skills. In reading, the eyes move from position to position, taking in information in discrete pauses which are separated by short jerking movements. During the movements, which last about 40 milliseconds, the page is blurred and little additional information is seen. Nevertheless, introspectively, reading appears to be a continuous task, and we are not aware of its jerky nature except when we observe someone else. The reason probably lies in the fact that the visual storage system can store information from the previous fixation while the eye moves. In reading, the problem of eye movements and of the detection and recognition of words is combined with the need to be able to manipulate linguistic symbols. In this sense, reading, listening, and speaking are all similar. Speech, however, involves information creation, and this represents an additional problem. In this section, the reading task will be used for analysis, but some of the results apply to listening and speaking as well.

In order to analyze reading it is necessary to consider both the input materials which are being used and the assigned output. Two tasks which appear similar but have quite different outputs are reading aloud and reading silently. Reading aloud is a much simpler task to analyze than silent reading. It requires conservation of the input information and thus has many properties in common with serial reaction-time tasks, in which only a change of code is required. Silent reading is far more complex because it is doubtful that complete retention is ever involved; the act of assimilating information is intermixed with information transformations of a very complex sort.

The input materials in reading can be analyzed at three quite different levels. The first is in terms of the statistical properties which control the order and frequency of the constituent words or letters. The second considers the syntactic properties of the grammar, which determine whether a given combination of elements is to be acceptable in a particular language. Finally, there are the semantic properties which concern the meaning asserted by a given statement. A certain amount of research on each of these levels has illustrated variables which affect the ability of man to manipulate language.

STATISTICAL LEVEL

At the statistical level it is possible to manipulate the degree to which a string of elements approximates those of a given language. Table 3 shows five strings of words which represent various orders of approximation to English. The zero order is random words chosen from a dictionary. The first order represents words chosen by their probability in English. The second and higher orders were collected from subjects in the following way: for the second order the subject was supplied with a common word which he had to use in a sentence. The word in the sentence immediately following the one which the subject was given became a member of the string and was supplied to a new subject who had to use it in a sentence. This process was continued until strings of any length were formed. The number of words supplied to the subjects was increased by one for each additional order and the same process was repeated. These strings are all nonsense, yet they are a special kind of nonsense since they preserve some of the sequential dependencies found in ordinary language.

Notice that the higher the order of approximation to English, the lower the amount of information per word. This may sound strange at first, but remember that information is related to uncertainty—and the more context, the less uncertainty. Thus, lower orders of approximation which represent high amounts of information are difficult to recognize when mixed with white noise. This is similar to the results obtained in recognizing words selected from populations of varying size (Figure 14). It is also easier to remember strings of words as the order of approximation to English increases. However, the increase in the number of words retained is not sufficient to balance the drop in information with order, so that more information, in the technical sense, is retained with lower orders.

It has been known for a long time that meaningful materials could be recognized and remembered better than nonsense materials.

Table 3

Word Strings of Varying Levels of Approximation to English
(After Miller and Selfridge, 1950)

Zero order
> Betwixt trumpeter pebbly complication vigorous tipple careen obscure attractive consequence expedition pene unpunished prominence chest sweetly basin awoke photographer ungrateful.

First order
> Tea realizing most so the together home and for were wanted to concert I posted he her it the walked.

Second order
> Sun was nice dormitory is I like chocolate cake but I think that book is he wants to school there.

Third order
> Family was large dark animal came roaring down the middle of my friends love books passionately very kiss is fine.

Fourth order
> Went to the movies with a man I used to go toward Harvard Square in Cambridge is mad fun for.

Fifth order
> Road in the country was insane especially in dreary rooms where they have some books to buy for studying Greek.

Seventh order
> Easy if you know how to crotchet you can make a simple scarf if they knew the color that it.

Prose text
> More attention has been paid to diet but mostly in relation to disease and to the growth of young children.

Work with approximations to English illustrates that some of this effect is due to the statistical nature of language. Languages are highly redundant; and redundant materials may lead to better performance in language just as in perceptual-motor skills. This is a significant point because the concept of meaning is a very important one in psychology, particularly with respect to language. The psychologist has the task of analyzing meaning into a number of simpler and more easily quantified variables. These experiments illustrate one aspect of meaning which has significant effects upon certain language tasks. It should not be expected, however, that the analysis of meaning and its role in human performance can stop with the statistical level. Some experiments (Coleman, 1963) have shown that even in memory tasks, performance with materials from prose text is better than the highest approximations. While the statistical nature of language explains some of the effects of meaning on human performance, it does not explain all of them. Moreover, memory and recognition are usually only a small part of language tasks. More often, language skills involve the ability to recognize similarity between different utterances.

SYNTACTIC LEVEL

According to one analysis (Miller and McKean, 1964, p. 297) a central task of the psychology of language is

to account for the fact that the people who know a language can deal with an unlimited variety of novel utterances in it. On the basis of a very finite exposure, a normal child quickly acquires an ability to understand and to produce admissible utterances that are different in form and content from any that he has ever heard or spoken before. This ability to project from a finite corpus of actual utterances into an infinite set of potential utterances is what we should expect our psycholinguistic theories to explain.

This problem is not unlike that which was examined under the general area of "pattern recognition" in Chapter 4. The subject can treat many physically different stimuli as representing the same general class. In language, however, the basis of similarity cannot be in the relatively simple spatial transformations which were useful in describing man's ability to handle patterns. Rather, the transformations involve subtle aspects of the structure or grammar of a sentence.

Miller's work has demonstrated some of the dimensions along which sentences can be transformed. He considers a core or kernel sentence of the type "Bill hit the ball." The kernel sentence can be transformed by such grammatical operations as producing a negation, a passive, or a passive negative. Miller arranged a sentence-matching test where the time for a subject to make each of these transformations could be computed. The average times for making a transformation between each of the sentence forms are shown in Figure 39. Notice that the values that require subjects to move along the edge of the figure are lower than those which require movement through the center. The transformations that go through the center may be thought of as requiring two steps. For example, kernel to passive negative may be viewed first as kernel to passive, and then passive to passive negative. In fact, the sum of these two operations yields a value of 2.7, which is identical to the direct transformation from kernel to passive negative. This exact

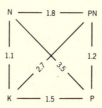

Figure 39

The time it takes (in seconds) to perform various grammatical transformations. K represents a kernel sentence. The various transformations are as follows: N, negative; P, passive; PN, passive negative. (Adapted from Miller, G. A., "Some Psychological Studies of Grammar," American Psychologist, 17 (1962), Copyright 1962 by the American Psychological Association and reproduced by permission.)

correspondence does not always occur in subsequent studies, but, in general, the time taken for a transformation that would require two steps in this scheme is longer than the time taken for one-step transformations. These results indicate that subjects can quickly spot the relation between a transformed sentence and its original and that the time taken to do so mirrors the complexity of the transformation and gives hints as to the types of rules involved. This type of switching between grammatical codes is highly similar to information-conserving transformations in perceptual-motor skills. The number of steps plays somewhat the same role as compatibility in choice RT.

Miller has also suggested that the subject tends to store sentences as a kernel plus a tag. According to this view, when a passive sentence is presented, the subject actually tends to retain the kernel corresponding to that sentence and a rule which tells him how to transform it at the time of recall. This speculation receives some support from studies of the learning and retention of transformed sentences, but may not be true in detail. In fact, the form of storage of simple digits and consonants is by no means settled. This is even more true of complex linguistic materials.

It is clear that the subject does have the ability to see that statements having common syntactic dimensions are related. His speed of transformation can be used to assess the relative difficulty of these learned relationships.

While it is important to be able to convert sentences into varying syntactic forms, a more important aspect of language behavior is the ability to recognize two sentences as having the same meaning. In a recent study, Miller and McKean (1964) found the rate at which subjects could recognize two sentences with different syntactic forms as having the same meaning—for example, "He caught her" and "She was caught by him." The experiment showed that the time it took to recognize that two such sentences had the same meaning was predictable from the time it took to make the transformation from one syntactic form into another. This evidence indicates that the processes subjects use in recognizing a common meaning in two sentences of different grammatical form is somewhat similar to the processes they use in transforming one form to the other.

SEMANTIC LEVEL

The recent Miller experiments, which consider man's ability to recognize similar meaning in different sentences, are closely related to the semantic level.

The statistical and syntactic levels tell us something about the organization of language. The major problem of understanding silent reading, however, lies not with sequential constraints or grammatical rules, but with the semantic level. While statistical constraints capture something about meaning for the purpose of memory, and grammatical rules represent something about how sentences may be made to mean the same things although in different forms, the semantic level plays the major role in the analysis of meaning as related to the task of comprehension. When we say that a subject comprehends the information, we mean that he can use it in a variety of different forms or can correctly evaluate new information in the light of the old.

When someone asserts that he remembers what is in a book or story, he does not mean that he can reproduce all or any part of it in ordered recall. Rather, he means that he can state the main ideas, relationships, or concepts asserted by the story.

In coming to understand materials of this sort, the subject must impose upon the words he hears or sees transformations which include selection, combination, and classification. To the extent that such transformations are involved, they should be manifested, as in other tasks, in the reduction of the rate at which the information can be assimilated. That is, the requirement to transform information will require a portion of the central processing mechanisms which will then be unavailable for dealing with new information from the story.

Poulton (1958b) investigated the effect of increasing the rate of presentation in reading. He was interested in comparing recall of specific words (pure retention) with a task where the subject had to select whether a new statement had the same meaning as one which had appeared in his previous reading material. The first task approximates information conservation, since it requires virtually complete recall, although Poulton did not require preservation of the order of the information. The second task clearly allows more opportunity for classification and transformation to occur, since the only requirement is to select a statement of similar meaning. For example, if the original statement had been "Surrealism is modern painting," the subject might be asked to say whether the statement "Surrealism is a recent art" has a meaning similar to the original. Clearly, if the subject had understood the original statement the new sentence would be seen as closely related. The subjects were required to read at rates of 293, 146, 73, and 37 words per minute. What is important for this discussion is that increasing the rate of reading resulted in significantly less material understood, as measured by the ability of subjects to select statements with the same meaning, but did not have as great an effect upon the recall of words.

Poulton concludes:

> These results suggest that there is a limit to the amount of material which can be understood in a given time. If we proceed faster than this we may be able to recall slightly more words, but we shall not be able to recall more meaning. To use the terminology of information theory, the rate of coding the information in reading appears to have an upper limit, which is reached before the rate at which information can be stored in an uncoded form. (p. 243)

Can anything more be said about the nature of the transformation processes which may underlie the subject's ability to perform Poulton's task? One way of viewing such processes is to consider each sentence as a miniature concept-learning situation. A declarative sentence may be viewed as establishing a relationship between the elements or sets which comprise it. Consider the statement "All scientists and some others support the test ban." The sentence posits an inclusion relationship between the set "test-ban supporters" and the set "scientists." If the subject comprehends this relationship, there are a number of new questions which he can now answer. For example, he knows that the statement "Some scientists reject the test ban" is false, while the statement "No scientists reject the ban" is true. By comprehending the original sentence, he is able to transfer its relationship to answer new questions. Notice that comprehension is not the same as memory. A subject may remember the original wording, but not be able to transfer its meaning, or the reverse. Comprehension is not an all-or-none process. Comprehension depends upon the extent of the subject's ability to transfer the original concept. He may be able to use the information to answer some questions, but not others. Of course, not all sentences are as unambiguous as the example about the test ban. Many sentences do not, by themselves, allow evaluation of other questions. However, sentences are not read in isolation, but include a context which usually serves to decrease the ambiguity.

If this analysis of comprehension is correct it should follow that the structure of sets developed by some sentences should be more difficult to comprehend than others. A series of experiments by Dawes (1964, 1966) considers this possibility. Dawes suggests four types of relationships between two sets: inclusion, exclusion, identity, and disjunction or overlap. The first three relations are called *nested*, since one set is wholly inside or wholly outside of the other. Only in the last type do the two concepts overlap. Dawes considers two types of errors. In one error the relationship is simplified because a disjunction is retained as nested. For example, one may be told that "Some revolutionaries are communists," but thereafter one may identify *all* revolutionaries as communists. This error is called *overgeneralization* and serves to reduce the information load in memory by distorting the actual relation between the sets. The opposite error is retaining a nested category as disjunctive. That is, having been told that all scientists support the test ban, the subject now distinguishes between scientists who do and scientists who do not support it. This error increases the complication of the relationship and is called a *pseudodiscrimination*. The subject makes a discrimination where the original statement does not allow for it.

If the analysis of man as a limited processing system is correct, he must simplify the information he reads or hears if he is to store substantial parts of it. Such simplifications may or may not result in error, depending upon the form of response required of the subject. However, errors which occur should more frequently be in the direction of simplification because of the nature of man's limited capacity to store untransformed information. This suggests that errors will more often be overgeneralizations than pseudodiscriminations.

Several experiments based on this analysis have been conducted. (Dawes, 1964, 1966). The stimulus material consists of stories of which *Circle Island* is an example. The story can be analyzed into sets

Circle Island
[*after Dawes, 1964*]

Circle Island is located in the middle of the Atlantic Ocean; it is a flat island with large grass meadows, good soil, but few rivers and hence a shortage of water.

The main occupations on the island are farming and cattle ranching. While the majority of the islanders are farmers, the ranchers are much more prosperous, for they are less affected by the lack of water; thus, no ranchers farm in addition.

The island is run democratically; all issues are decided by a majority vote of the islanders. The actual governing body is a 10-man senate, whose job is to carry out the will of the majority. Since the most desirable trait in a senator is administrative ability, the senate consists of the 10 best proven administrators—the island's ten richest men. For years, all the senators have been ranchers.

Recently, an island scientist discovered a cheap method of converting salt water into fresh water; as a result, some of the island farmers wanted to build a canal across the island, so that they could use the water from the canal to cultivate the island's central region. Some of the farmers formed a pro canal association and even persuaded a few senators to join.

The pro canal association brought the idea of constructing a canal to a vote. All the islanders voted, with all the members of the pro canal association and all the farmers voting for construction and everybody else voting against it. The majority voted in favor of construction.

The senate, however, decided it would be too dangerous having a canal that was more than 2 inches wide and 3 inches deep. After starting construction on such a canal, the island engineers found no water would flow into it and the project had to be abandoned.

(A diagram of the set relations in this story is presented in Fig. 40.)

with various relationships. Figure 40 shows an analysis of the story. After subjects have read the story, they are required to answer questions. The questions ascertain the subject's retention of the relationships between the various sets. These experiments show that a considerable number of errors in retention are made, and that the errors tend to be overgeneralizations more frequently than pseudodiscriminations. That is, the subjects have a tendency to collapse disjunctive relationships into simpler inclusions, exclusions, or identities.

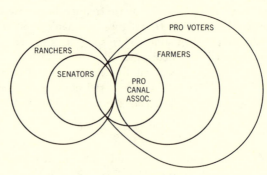

Figure 40

A diagram representing the set relationships in the story of Circle Island. (After Dawes, 1964.)

This work on comprehension of written materials is only a start toward an understanding of the nature of comprehension. However, enough is known to demonstrate that the issues of comprehension are more complex than simple memory. An analysis of comprehension must include some account of transformation processes, memory, and their interaction. Many of the limitations in man's processing capacities can be seen to apply directly to this situation.

SUMMARY

This chapter has dealt with the analysis of language skills. Two fundamental components were considered. The first component involved transformations which could be information conserving, reducing, or creating. It was suggested that the size of a transformation is related to the rate and accuracy with which it can be performed. The second component was the memory or storage of information relevant to the task. These two components interact because previously stored material competes for central capacity with new input. The greater the size of the transformation upon incoming input, the more loss from short-term memory will take place.

In the light of the interaction between memory and thought, the complex tasks of reading, listening, and speaking were considered. It was argued that seemingly similar tasks could demand different types of processing from man. For example, reading aloud is an information-conserving situation while reading silently requires many information-reducing transformations. At the statistical, syntactic, and semantic levels, efforts were made to show how the constraints inherent in language structure affect the processes of memory and transformation involved in various tasks. An attempt was made to define comprehension in terms of the ability to transfer a concept presented in a sentence to new situations. The ability of man to comprehend large quantities of information depends upon his ability to impose appropriate transformations.

APPLICATIONS

8

Technology is continually placing new demands upon man's performance capacities. Within the time it takes for a human being simply to react to a stimulus, a high-speed airplane can travel hundreds of feet. Cars approach each other in the highway at rates of 150 miles per hour and, during the brief time it takes for the gap to close, a driver must exercise absolute judgment about the safety of passing the car in front of him. Factories require inspectors to detect defective items occurring no more often than once in 10,000 times. The telephone system requires that we retain up to ten digits long enough to dial a number in another city. A military officer, a politician, an executive, or a juror is required to make decisions involving great masses of data which must be assimilated and reflected in the final choice.

Man has always had to learn new skills in order to adapt to his environment. The twentieth century is unique, however, in both the rapidity with which such adjustments are required and the stress which they place upon human capacity. These developments have forced psychologists into showing an interest in the problems of redesigning the environment so that the best use can be made of human abilities. This chapter offers a few illustrations to show how the principles of human performance developed in this book can be applied to these problems. While the space remaining will hardly be adequate to do justice to the topic, many other good sources exist which for the interested reader will supplement this discussion (Bennett, Degan, and Spiegel, 1963; Chapanis, 1965).

The first example involves one of our most familiar systems. Using the telephone is a daily experience. Occasionally an error is made in dialing, usually with only slight inconvenience to the caller, although often more annoying to the party mistakenly called. The telephone company has an annual bill of many millions of dollars due to wrong numbers. Moreover, the development of direct long-distance dialing has greatly increased this cost while placing additional burden upon man's memory capacity.

The psychologist can assist in the design of this system so as to reduce error. Dialing a new telephone number is related to the ability to store information in short-term memory. One recent study indicates a very simple and effective method of improving this process. A phone number consists of two different parts. The prefix contains relatively little information and is highly familiar. Within a single city, only a limited number of prefixes are used and, even with the addition of direct long-distance dialing, the numbers most people call have relatively few different prefixes. The remainder of the digits, on the other hand, change completely with every individual number called. Since the probability that a given prefix will be used is much greater than that of the remainder of the number, the amount of information in the prefix is lower. Shepard and Sheenan (1965) reasoned that a long storage time for the prefix would not be as harmful as long storage time for the high-information parts of the number. This notion corresponds with laboratory studies which show that three letters forming a familiar word result in much less loss over time than do three unrelated letters. A study was conducted to compare the standard dialing procedure with one in which the prefix was dialed last, storage time for the remainder of the number being thereby reduced. The new method led to a drop in errors of almost 50 per cent.

Another simple technique for improving a common industrial task involves the maintenance of alertness when a man is required to monitor products for small departures from acceptable quality. In Chapter 3 it was noted that in such *vigilance tasks* effectiveness in detecting a signal will decline with the time spent on the task. The deleterious effect of time increases as the probability of actually finding a target is reduced. That is, the decrement over time is greater for detecting rare targets than for detecting frequent ones. Psychologists have sought to improve this situation by increasing the number of targets which the subject must detect and by introducing the powerful motivating force that a knowledge of results provides (Baker, 1960). This is done by putting in some deliberately defective items. Since these false targets have been deliberately inserted, they can be built to trigger a warning device if they are missed by the monitor. This technique serves to reduce errors on the genuine targets.

For some skills it is difficult to select an appropriate measure of task performance as aspects of the situation vary. As an example, consider the task of driving an automobile. Traffic patterns, mechanical conditions, and changes in the interior design of automobiles should all have some effect on driving efficiency. But it is not obvious how to measure these effects. For one thing, driving skill is so highly developed that gross performance continues to be adequate within a great variety of conditions. Moreover, the exact timing and sequence of movements appropriate to driving change under different conditions. In order to handle this problem, some psychologists have sought to apply the principles of man's limited processing capacity. This is done by adding a numerical task to the primary driving task. Subjects are required to perform the numerical task under different vehicular and traffic conditions. Several studies (e.g., Brown and Poulton, 1961) have shown performance on the numerical task changes as the driving task demands varying amounts of the available capacity of the subjects. By means of this technique innovations in vehicular design can be explored and their effects compared.

The examples given so far involve rather simple applications of basic principles of performance. The purpose has been the improvement in the design or the assessment of equipment or of a system. The final example will be more complicated. It involves the ability of people to make decisions. This is a new area of research and promises to be important in the future.

Consider a juror who must decide upon the innocence or guilt of a defendant. Each witness, or perhaps each fact testified to by a witness, is an item of information which may cause the juror's impression about the guilt or innocence of the defendant to change.

Research on decision making in situations analogous to that of a jury has shown that different orders of presentation may lead to different opinions (Anderson, 1959). This finding is hardly in accord with the usual notion of justice, by which the question of innocence or guilt should not be dependent on the order in which the evidence is presented. Why does order make a difference? One reason is related to the inaccuracy of the juror's memory. He cannot retain all the information he has received during a trial. A second factor has to do with the properties of selective attention. As has been shown in Chapter 4, subjects have considerable facility for emphasizing one or another aspect of incoming information; which aspects get emphasized depends upon the hypotheses directing the subjects' attention. As a trial unfolds, new hypotheses may be suggested which shift the apparent relevance of this or that aspect of the case. However, the juror cannot go backward in time to reguide his attention. Material which has not been attended to cannot be recalled.

In addition to the effect of order, another aspect of man's capacity to process information—namely, his tendency to resist changing his mind in the light of new evidence (Edwards, Lindman, and Phillips, 1965)—affects his decision-making ability. This means that in comparison to an optimal statistical model for revising opinion, men tend to extract less information than they might from each new piece of evidence. The extent of men's conservatism in this regard is proportional to the impact which the information ought to have. The greater the potential impact, the more conservative human performance is. This should not be too surprising if you consider decision making to be one type of information-reduction task. As evidence accumulates the uncertainty of the subject about the correct decisions tends to be reduced. Evidence which has a big impact requires a large amount of information reduction, and (just as in other information-processing tasks) as the amount of information reduction increases, so does the difficulty of the task (Posner, 1965). This effect shows up in an increasing inability to extract as much information as the evidence will allow.

In one laboratory study (Peterson, Schneider, and Miller, 1965), when 48 items of evidence were presented simultaneously, the subjects revised their estimates no more than they would have if only 12 items had been presented, and only twice as much as if only one item had been presented. This indicates that subjects become more conservative as the amount of information they are required to assimilate increases—a finding which suggests another way in which information processing tends to violate the usual notions of justice. Ordinarily we would think that guilt or innocence should not to be affected by the way in which information is packaged. But the study just cited suggests that the same information presented in a large block may have less impact than if it were presented more slowly.

Recently (Edwards et al., 1965), psychologists have begun to make proposals concerning the design of systems which would reduce errors imposed by the natural limitations of man as an information processor. These proposals would require men to make a number of serial decisions based on restricted aspects of the evidence, rather than a single global decision. It has also been proposed that computers be used to combine the successive human judgments in such a way as to reduce the conservatism apparent in man's decision making. Although such suggestions are in the formative stage, they may, if further research should support their use, serve as supplements in man's effort to reach decisions which are not unduly influenced by limitations in his own processing abilities.

In these and other ways, it is evident that the study of human performance holds great promise for the development of a technology which will provide the means for using man's capacities to his maximum benefit.

REFERENCES

Alpern, M., Lawrence, M. and Wolsk, D. *Sensory processes*. Belmont, Calif.: Brooks/Cole, Wadsworth, a division of, 1967.

Anderson, Nancy S. Poststimulus cuing in immediate memory. *J. exp. Psychol.*, 1960 *60*, 216–221.

Anderson, N. Test of a model for opinion change. *J. abnorm. soc. Psychol.*, 1959, *59*, 371–381.

Attneave, F. *Applications of information theory to psychology*. New York: Holt, 1959.

_____. Perception and related areas. In S. Koch (ed.), *Psychology: A study of a science*, Vol. 4. New York: McGraw-Hill, 1963.

Averbach, E. The span of apprehension as a function of exposure duration. *J. verb. Learning verb. Behavior*, 1963, *2*, 60–64.

Bahrick, H. P. An analysis of stimulus variables influencing the proprioceptive control of movement. *Psychol. Rev.*, 1957, *64*, 324–328.

_____. Noble, M., and Fitts, P. M. Extra-task performance as a measure of learning a primary task. *J. exp. Psychol.*, 1954, *48*, 298–302.

Baker, C. H. Maintaining the level of vigilance by artificial signals. *J. appl. Psychol.*, 1960, *44*, 336–338.

Bartlett, F. C. *Thinking: An experimental and social study*. New York: Basic Books, 1958.

Bennett, E., Degan, J., and Spiegel, J. *Human factors in technology*. New York: McGraw-Hill, 1963.

Birmingham, H. P., and Taylor, F. V. Human engineering approach to the design of man-operated continuous control systems. *Naval Research Laboratory Rept. No. 4333*, April, 1954.

Boring, E. G. *History of experimental psychology*. New York: Appleton-Century-Crofts, 1950.

Boynton, R. Some temporal factors in vision. In W. A. Rosenblith (ed.), *Sensory communication*. New York: Wiley, 1961.

Brainard, R. W., Irby, T. S., Fitts, P. M., and Alluisi, E. A. Some variables influencing the rate of gain of information. *J. exp. Psychol.*, 1962, *63*, 105–110.

Broadbent, D. E. *Perception and communication*. New York: Pergamon Press, 1958.

_____. Flow of information within the organism. *J. verb. Learn. verb. Behav.*, 1963a, *2*, 34–39.

——————. Differences and interaction between stresses. *Quart. J. exp. Psychol.*, 1963b, *15*, 205–211.

——————. S-R compatibility and the processing of information. *Acta Psychologica*, 1964, *23*, 325–326.

Broadhurst, P. L. Emotionality and the Yerkes-Dodson law. *J. exp. Psychol.*, 1957, *54*, 345–352.

Brown, I. D., and Poulton, E. C. Measuring the spare "mental capacity" of car drivers by a subsidiary task. *Ergonomics*, 1961, *5*, 35–40.

Bruner, J. Going beyond the information given. In *Contemporary approaches to cognition*. Cambridge, Mass.: Harvard Univ. Press, 1957.

Bryan, W. L., and Harter, N. Studies on the telegraphic language: The acquisition of a hierarchy of habits. *Psychol. Rev.*, 1899, *6*, 345–375.

Buschke, H. Retention in immediate memory estimated without retrieval. *Science*, 1963, *140*, 56–57.

Buswell, G. T. An experimental study of the eye-voice span in reading. *Suppl. educ. Monogr.*, 1927, *17*.

Butsch, R. L. C. Eye movements and the eye-hand span in typewriting. *J. educ. Psychol.*, 1932, *23*, 104–121.

Butter, C. M. *Neuropsychology: The study of brain and behavior*. Belmont, Calif.: Brooks/Cole, Wadsworth, a division of, pending.

Chapanis, A. *Man-machine engineering*. Belmont, Calif.: Wadsworth, 1965.

Chase, W. G., and Posner, M. I. The effect of auditory and visual confusability on visual and memory search tasks. Paper presented to the Midwestern Psychological Association, Chicago, Illinois; May 1, 1965 (unpublished).

Cheatham, P. G., and White, C. T. Temporal numerosity: III. Auditory perception of number. *J. exp. Psychol.*, 1954, *47*, 425–428.

Cherry, E. C. Some experiments on the recognition of speech, with one and with two ears. *J. acoust. Soc. Amer.*, 1953, *25*, 975–979.

——————, and Taylor, W. K. Some further experiments upon the recognition of speech, with one and with two ears. *J. acoust. Soc. Amer.*, 1954, *26*, 554–559.

Cofer, C. N., and Appley, M. H. *Motivation: Theory and research*. New York: Wiley, 1964.

Coleman, E. B. Approximations to English: Some comments on the method. *Amer. J. Psychol.*, 1963, *76*, 239–247.

Conover, D. W. The amount of information in the absolute judgement of Munsell Hues. *WADC Tech. Note 58-262*, 1959.

Conrad, R. Very brief delay of immediate recall. *Quart. J. exp. Psychol.*, 1960, *12*, 45–47.

——————. Practice, familiarity, and reading rate for words and nonsense syllables. *Quart. J. exp. Psychol.*, 1962, *14*, 71–76.

Craik, K. J. W.   Theory of the human operator in control systems: II. Man as an element in a control system. *Brit. J. Psychol.*, 1948, *38*, 142–148.

Creamer, L. R.   Event uncertainty, psychological refractory period, and human data processing. *J. exp. Psychol.*, 1963, *66*, 187–194.

Crook, M. N., Harker, G. S., Hoffman, A. C., and Kennedy, J. L.   Effect of amplitude of apparent vibration, brightness, and type size on numerical reading. Medford, Mass.: The Institute for Applied Experimental Psychology, Tufts College; *AF technical report No. 5246*, 1950.

Crossman, E. R. F. W.   The measurement of discriminability. *Quart. J. exp. Psychol.*, 1955, *7*, 176–195.

──────────. A theory of the acquisition of speed-skill. *Ergonomics*, 1959, *2*, 153–166.

──────────. The information capacity of the human motor system in pursuit tracking. *Quart. J. exp. Psychol.*, 1960a, *12*, 1–16.

──────────. Information and serial order in human immediate memory. In C. Cherry, (ed.), *Information theory*. London: Butterworth, 1960b.

Crowder, R. G.   Verbal short-term memory as a function of degree of learning on a perceptual-motor interpolated activity. *Univ. Michigan Technical Report*, December, 1964.

Davis, R.   The human operator as a single channel information system. *Quart. J. exp. Psychol.*, 1957, *9*, 119–129.

Dawes, R. M.   Cognitive distortion. *Psychol. Reports*, 1964, *14*, 443–459.

──────────. Memory and distortion of meaningful written material. *Brit. J. Psychol.*, 1966, *57*, 77–86.

Edwards, W., Lindman, H., and Phillips, L.   Emerging technologies for making decisions. In T. Newcomb (ed.), *New directions in psychology*, Vol. 2. New York: Holt, Rinehart, and Winston, 1965.

Elkind, J. I., and Sprague, L. T.   Transmission of information in simple manual control systems. *IRE Transactions of the PGHFE*, 1961, *2*, 58–60.

Fenn, W. O.   The mechanics of muscular contraction in man. *J. appl. Physics*, 1938, *9*, 165–177.

Fitts, P. M.   The information capacity of the human motor system in controlling the amplitude of movement. *J. exp. Psychol.*, 1954, *47*, 381–391.

──────────. Perceptual-motor skill learning. In A. W. Melton, (ed.), *Categories of human learning*, New York: Academic Press, 1964.

──────────. Human information processing: Applications of information measures. In *Human factors engineering*. Ann Arbor, Mich.: Univ. Michigan, 1964.

──────────. Cognitive aspects of information processing: III. Set for speed vs. accuracy. *J. exp. Psychol.*, 1966, *71*, 849–857.

──────────, and Biederman, I.   SR compatibility and information reduction. *J. exp. Psychol.*, 1965, *69*, 408–412.

—————, and Deininger, R. L. SR compatibility: Correspondence among paired elements within stimulus and response codes. *J. exp. Psychol.*, 1954, *48*, 483–492.

—————, and Peterson, J. R. Information capacity of discrete motor responses. *J. exp. Psychol.*, 1964, *67*, 103–112.

—————, Peterson, J. R., and Wolpe, G. Cognitive aspects of information processing: II. Adjustments to stimulus redundancy. *J. exp. Psychol.*, 1963, *65*, 423–432.

—————, and Seeger, C. M. SR compatibility: Spatial characteristics of stimulus and response codes. *J. exp. Psychol.*, 1953, *46*, 199–210.

—————, and Switzer, Gail. Cognitive aspects of information processing: I. The familiarity of SR sets and subsets. *J. exp. Psychol.*, 1962, *63*, 321–329.

Freeman, F. N. *The teaching of handwriting.* Boston: Houghton Mifflin, 1914.

Garner, W. R. *Uncertainty and structure as psychological concepts.* New York: Wiley, 1962.

Glanville, A. D., and Dallenbach, K. M. The range of attention. *Amer. J. Psychol.*, 1920, *41*, 207–236.

Goldman-Eisler, Frieda. The predictability of words in context and the length of pauses in speech. *Language and speech*, 1958, *1*, 226–231.

Gould, J. D. Differential visual feedback of component motions. *J. exp. Psychol.*, 1965, *69*, 263–268.

Hartman, E. B. The influence of practice and pitch-distance between tones on the absolute identification of pitch. *Amer. J. Psychol.*, 1954, *67*,1–14.

Hebb, D. The American revolution. *Amer. Psychologist*, 1960, *15*, 735–745.

Helson, H. *Adaptation-level theory.* New York: Harper, 1964.

Hick, W. E. Reaction time for the amendment of a response. *Quart. J. exp. Psychol.*, 1948, *1*, 175–179.

—————. On the rate of gain of information. *Quart. J. exp. Psychol.*, 1952, *4*, 11–26.

Hirsh, I. J., and Sherrick, C. E. Perceived order in different sense modalities. *J. exp. Psychol.*, 1961, *62*, 423–432.

Hyman, R. Stimulus information as a determinant of reaction time. *J. exp. Psychol.*, 1953, *45*, 188–196.

Keller, F. S. The phantom plateau. *J. exp. anal. Behav.*, 1958, *1*, 1–13.

Keppel, G., and Underwood, B. J. Proactive inhibition in short-term retention of single items. *J. verb. learn. verb. Behav.*, 1962, *1*, 153–161.

Klemmer, E. T. Simple reaction time as a function of time uncertainty. *J. exp. Psychol.*, 1957, *54*, 195–200.

—————. Communication and human performance. *Human factors*, 1962, *4*, 75–79.

——————, and Frick, F. C. Assimilation of information from dot and matrix patterns. *J. exp. Psychol.*, 1953, *45*, 15–19.

Koch, H. L. A neglected phase of the part/whole problem. *J. exp. Psychol.*, 1923, *6*, 366–376.

Leonard, J. A. Tactual choice reactions. *Quart. J. exp. Psychol.*, 1959, *11*, 76–83.

Lloyd, K. E., Reid, L. S., and Feallock, J. B. Short-term retention as a function of the average number of items presented. *J. exp. Psychol.*, 1960, *60*, 201–207.

Mace, C. A. Homeostasis, needs and values. *Brit. J. Psychol.*, 1953, *44*, 200–210.

Mackworth, Jane F. Performance decrement in vigilance, threshold, and high speed perceptual motor tasks. *Canad. J. Psychol.*, 1964, *18*, 209–223.

Melton, A. W. Implications of short-term memory for a general theory of memory. *J. verb. Learn. verb. Behav.*, 1963, *2*, 1–22.

Merkel, J. Die zeitlichen Verhaltnisse der Willensthatigkeit. *Philos. St.*, 1885, *2*, 73–127.

Miller, G. A. *Language and communication.* New York: McGraw-Hill, 1951.

——————. The magical number seven plus or minus two: Some limits on our capacity for processing information. *Psychol. Rev.*, 1956, *63*, 81–97.

——————. Some psychological studies of grammar. *Amer. Psychologist*, 1962, *17*, 748–762.

——————, Heise, G. A., and Lichten, W. The intelligibility of speech as a function of the context of the materials. *J. exp. Psychol.*, 1951, *41*, 329–335.

——————, and McKean, Kathryn O. A chronometric study of some relations between sentences. *Quart. J. exp. Psychol.*, 1964, *16*, 297–308.

——————, and Selfridge, J. A. Verbal context and the recall of meaningful material. *Amer. J. Psychol.*, 1950, *63*, 176–185.

Miller, J. G. Adjusting to overloads of information. In D. McK. Rioch and E. A. Weinstein (eds.), *Disorders of communication.* Research Publications, Assoc. Res. Nerv. Ment. Dis., 1964, *42*, 87–100.

Morin, R. E., and Grant, D. A. Learning and performance of a key-pressing task as a function of the degree of spatial stimulus-response correspondence, *J. exp. Psychol.*, 1955, *49*, 39–47.

Mowbray, G. H. Choice reaction time for skilled responses. *Quart. J. exp. Psychol.*, 1960, *12*, 193–202.

——————, and Rhoades, M. U. On the reduction of choice-reaction times with practice. *Quart. J. exp. Psychol.*, 1959, *11*, 16–23.

Murdock, B. B. The retention of individual items. *J. exp. Psychol.*, 1961, *62*, 618–625.

Neisser, U., Novick, R., and Lazar, R. Searching for ten targets simultaneously. *Perceptual and motor skills*, 1963, *17*, 955-961.

Paillard, J. The patterning of skilled movements. In *Handbook of Physiology*, Vol. III. Washington, D.C.: Am. Physio. Soc., 1960, 1679-1708.

Peterson, C. R., Schneider, R. J., and Miller, A. J. Sample size and the revision of subjective probabilities. *J. exp. Psychol.*, 1965, *69*, 522-527.

Peterson, L. R., and Peterson, Margaret. Short-term retention of individual items. *J. exp. Psychol.*, 1959, *58*, 193-198.

Pew, R. W. Temporal factors limiting serial performance. Unpublished paper. Univ. Michigan, 1963.

—————. Timing accuracy over short intervals. Unpublished paper. Univ. Michigan, 1965.

Pierce, J. R., and Karlin, J. E. Reading rates and the information rate of a human channel. *Bell Sys. Tech. J.*, 1957, *36*, 497-516.

Pollack, I. The information of elementary auditory displays, I. *J. acoust. Soc. Amer.*, 1952, *24*, 745-749.

—————. Verbal reaction times to briefly presented words. *Perceptual and motor skills*, 1963, *17*, 137-138.

—————, and Ficks, L. Information of multidimensional auditory displays. *J. acoust. Soc. Amer.*, 1954, *26*, 155-158.

—————, Johnson, L. D., and Knaff, R. P. Running memory span. *J. exp. Psychol.*, 1959, *57*, 137-146.

Posner, M. I. An informational approach to thinking. *Univ. Michigan technical report, O 2814*, 1962.

—————. Uncertainty as a predictor of similarity in the study of generalization. *J. exp. Psychol.*, 1964a, *63*, 113-118.

—————. Information reduction in the analysis of sequential tasks. *Psychol. Rev.*, 1964b, *71*, 491-504.

—————. Memory and thought in human intellectual performance. *Brit. J. Psychol.*, 1965, *56*, 197-215.

—————, and Rossman, E. The effect of size and location of informational transforms upon short-term retention. *J. exp. Psychol.*, 1965, *70*, 496-505.

Poulton, E. C. Anticipation in open and closed sensorimotor skills. Medical Research Council. *SPU Rpt. No. 138/50*. September, 1950.

—————. Copying behind during dictation. *Quart. J. exp. Psychol.* 1958a, *10*, 48-55.

—————. Time for reading and memory. *Brit. J. Psychol.*, 1958b, *49*, 230-245.

—————. Sequential short-term memory: Some tracking experiments. *Ergonomics*, 1963, *6*, 117-132.

Quastler, H., and Wulff, V. J. Human performance in information transmission. *Control Systems Laboratory Report No. 62*, Univ. Illinois, 1955.

Seibel, R. Discrimination reaction time for a 1,023 alternative task. *J. exp. Psychol.*, 1963, *66*, 215–226.

Shannon, C. E., and Weaver, W. *The mathematical theory of communication.* Urbana, Ill: Univ. Illinois Press, 1949.

Shepard, R. N. Production of constrained associates and the informational uncertainty of the constraint. *Amer. J. Psychol.*, 1963, *76*, 218–228.

—————, Hovland, C. I., and Jenkins, H. M. Learning and memorization of classifications. *Psychological Monog.*, 1961, 75, Whole No. 517.

—————, and Sheenan, Maureen M. Immediate recall of numbers containing a familiar prefix or postfix. *Perceptual and motor skills*, 1965, *21*, 263–273.

—————, and Teghtsoonian, Martha. Retention of information under conditions approaching a steady state. *J. exp. Psychol.*, 1961, *62*, 302–309.

Smith, K. U., and Smith, W. M. *Perception and motion.* Philadelphia: W. B. Saunders, 1962.

Smode, A. Learning and performance in a tracking task under two levels of achievement information feedback. *J. exp. Psychol.*, 1958, *56*, 297–304.

Snoddy, G. S. Learning and stability. *J. appl. Psychol.*, 1926, *10*, 1–36.

Sperling, G. The information available in brief visual presentations. *Psychol. Monog.*, 1960, *74*, Whole No. 498.

—————. A model for visual memory tasks. *Human factors*, 1963, *5*, 19–31.

Stevens, J. C., and Savin, H. B. On the form of learning curves. *J. exp. anal. Behav.*, 1962, *5*, 15–18.

Stratton, G. M. Vision without inversion of the retinal image. *Psychol. Rev.*, 1897, *4*, 341–481.

Swets, J. A. Signal detection and recognition by human observers. New York: Wiley, 1964.

Triesman, Anne. Verbal responses and contextual constraints in language. *J. verb. Learn. verb. Behav.*, 1965, *4*, 118–128.

Underwood, B. J., Runquist, W. N., and Schultz, R. W. Response learning in paired-associate lists as a function of intralist similarity. *J. exp. Psychol.*, 1959, *58*, 70–78.

Von Helmholtz, H. On the rate of transmission of the nerve impulse. Translated in W. Dennis (ed.), *Readings in the history of psychology.* New York: Appleton-Century-Crofts, 1948, 197–198.

Walker, E. L. *Conditioning and instrumental learning.* Belmont, California: Brooks/Cole, Wadsworth, a division of, 1967.

Warrick, M. J. The psychological refractory period, disparate stimuli and responses. Unpublished doctoral dissertation, Ohio State Univ., 1961.

—————. Kibler, A. W., Topmiller, D. A., and Bates, C. Response time to unexpected stimuli. *Amer. Psychologist*, 1964, *19*, 528.

Welford, A. T. The psychological refractory period and timing of high speed performance: A review and a theory. *Brit. J. Psychol.*, 1952, *43*, 2–19.

Wertheimer, M. Drei Adhandlungen zur Gestalttheorie. Erlangen, Germany. Philosophischen Akademie, 1925.

White, B. W. Recognition of familiar characters under an unfamiliar transformation. *Perceptual and motor skills*, 1962, *15*, 107–116.

White, C. T. Temporal numerosity and the psychological unit of duration. *Psychol. Monogr.*, 1963, 77, No. 12, Whole No. 575.

Woodworth, R. S. *Experimental psychology.* New York: Holt, 1938.

—————, and Schlosberg, H. *Experimental psychology.* New York: Holt, 1954.

NAME INDEX

SUBJECT INDEX